Fundamentals for Profit
in Undervalued Stocks

Every man who knows how to read
has it in his power to magnify
himself, to multiply the ways in
which he exists, to make his life
full, significant, and interesting.

—ALDOUS HUXLEY

Fundamentals for Profit in Undervalued Stocks

Louis Plotnick
Kevin M. McCrane

Englewood Cliffs, N.J.
PRENTICE-HALL, INC.

The observations, opinions and
conclusions made in this book are
those of the authors and should
not be construed as those of
Shearson, Hammill & Company.

LOUIS PLOTNICK

Louis Plotnick and Kevin M. Mc-Crane gained extensive experience in the fields of business management before becoming Registered Representatives of the New York Stock Exchange associated with Shearson, Hammill & Co. A deep knowledge of and insight into the intricacies of corporate operations suits the authors admirably to the daily process of applying the fundamentals and principles of the Undervalued Method to individual corporations and their stocks.

Fundamentals for Profit in Undervalued Stocks, featuring the Undervalued Method of stock evaluation, reflects the authors' broad business and financial backgrounds and is an extremely enlightening and valuable addition to the literature of the Stock Market.

Mr. Plotnick, a graduate of Long Island University, received his M.B.A. from New York University. Mr. McCrane is a graduate of Villanova University, B.S.

KEVIN McCRANE

Introduction

FUNDAMENTALS FOR PROFIT IN UNDERVALUED STOCKS is intended both to provide the investor with a valid method of investigating stocks before he invests, and to enable him to make money. The investor today happily has the ability to realize the possibilities for gain through investing in common stocks, and second, the opportunity to risk capital for these gains. He will be interested in studying a system designed to provide profit potential in the often overlooked area of "The Undervalueds."

The sheer size of the Stock Market, with the tremendous number of variables affecting the general market and each issue, offers a serious obstacle to understanding stock price movement. By subjecting a small segment of the market to thorough study it is anticipated that the investor will have a clear understanding not only of this segment of the market, but a broad understanding of what makes *all* stocks move.

The Undervalueds provides a fascinating group of stocks whose price movements can be forecast with a surprisingly high degree of success, although this book is not a tout book of current "hot" stocks, an effortless means of gaining success, or a substitute for judgment. It is a tool, however, for the alert investor and can considerably enhance his chances for success.

Many names and terms are used to describe stocks which have some element that will, or has caused them to, appreciate sharply in price. "Special Situations," "Underpriced," "great upside, small downside," etc. "The Undervalueds" must be accepted as a misnomer, utilized for lack of a better term. A misnomer because it is normally a hindsight-induced term alluding to a stock which has already appreciated in value. For the purposes of this book it suits particularly well the type of issues we have selected to demonstrate the validity of the method outlined for profit.

The issues used as examples are companies with basically simple capital structures engaged in varied industries which have, at one time or another, been in the position of selling at a very low price (usually for a good reason) but which have at that time telegraphed strong signals of change for the better.

The investor who is capable of using public information to find these issues, who has the understanding and ability to investigate published reports of the company involved, who can distill meaning from the facts discovered, and who can add to these an educated judgment, has the opportunity of making money and reducing risks of loss to near minimums.

That is the primary purpose of this book—to provide the means to accomplish these goals.

For example, "current ratio" is an important consideration in evaluation of a stock because it is an index to the financial ability of a company to pay its current obligations. An explanation of this term (and every other one used) as it relates to the risk involved in purchase of stock, or the price of the stock, is given along with the utilization of reports to glean meaningful information. This is an attempt to sweep away the mists of too often obscure terms and to *present an intelligible portrait of all stocks* through the delightful miniature of the Undervalueds.

Because there is risk in all investment it will be seen that much of this book is devoted to safe-guarding the usually hard–earned dollars of investors. Rules are detailed for purchase of the Undervalueds and the always present risks of loss are treated throughout the book. Concentration on profit can be self-defeating if constant surveillance of risks is neglected. The Undervalueds form a unique, always present group of securities which can provide the necessary "upside potential" and "downside protection."

Far reaching and long term benefits must accrue to the investor who achieves a "sense of stocks." The self-imposed rules of many investors which often serve to defeat them in their quest for profits will hopefully be dispelled through reading this book. For example, "Never buy at the high," "Put 'em away and forget 'em," "I can't sell with a loss," "My cousin knows a director and he says . . . ," "I won't sell with this profit. It's going higher," "My uncle gave this stock to me," "But it has such a good dividend." All of these reasons or lack of reason are sometimes valid, but presented here is an unemotional (if the investor can ever be said to be unemotional), factual means of using measurements of value in all stocks. It represents an opportunity for the investor to inquire "Why?" to every recommendation submitted to him, and the further comfort of being able, to a much greater extent, to distill fact from fancy, reason from emotion, and realism from dubious hope.

A series of steps which grow progressively more detailed are explained and demonstrated to enable the investor to use facts available, arrange them in effective order, and convert them to meaningful values. Upon completion of the work he may stand upon the pyramid so constructed and weigh possible risks against potential gain and arrive at a decision. The decision process is simplified to a great extent by the yardsticks provided, but there is room for the speculator to increase risk by dropping these bars or limits, and the conservative can reduce risk still further by raising them.

"The Undervalueds" further attempts to answer "When do I sell?" There is, of course, no attempt of claim that you can buy at the low or sell at the high. There is, however, a yardstick provided for helping to make the decisions.

The recognition of the hazards connected with all forms of investment precludes any attempt to eliminate risk. Because of the existence of dangers of loss in investing in common stocks it becomes all important for the investor to make use of as many facts as possible to restrict such losses. Insofar as it is possible to deal with near absolutes in a field which so abounds with variables, this book provides a foundation in the measurable items of stock purchases.

The secondary goal of the book is much broader in scope and recognizes that the stocks classified and examined as Undervalueds are merely extreme cases of a huge number of stocks which can be and are purchased for gain through the use of the principles detailed here. Every purchase of every stock is, in the final analysis, made in the belief that the stock is "undervalued." By using the "fundamental" approach to stock purchase the investor is capable of measuring the risk and estimating whether or not there are good chances for gain.

In short, this book provides a definite, measured, and measurable series of tests that can be applied to Undervalued stocks, gives methods of finding them, and is applicable ultimately to all stocks.

We are pleased to acknowledge our sincere gratitude to our families for their patience, assistance, and encouragement while the manuscript slowly took shape. Also, we readily admit our debt to the following persons: John F. Salisbury, David Heenehan, Harold Hahn, William Hartz, Gerson K. Plotnick, and Ruth M. Underwood, who helped us by their individual contributions to make this a more interesting and valuable book.

Contents

Fundamentals for Profit
in Undervalued Stocks

I

The Background of
the Undervalued Stock

An introduction to the special situations in the stock market called "Undervalueds" and the reasons why they exist and why they constitute a worthwhile pursuit.

Budget Finance Plan is a small loan company whose operations center on the West Coast. The stock of this company is traded on the American Stock Exchange. In January of 1961 Budget Finance (or BUG to use its trading symbol) was selling for $8.00 per share. One year later, in January of 1962, the stock was selling at $16.00 per share. A phenomenal rise? Not really. Other stocks have done much better in shorter periods of time. Sensational advances in price are newsworthy items for the financial pages of the daily papers. What makes BUG a worthy introduction for this book?

THE CHIEF QUALIFICATION OF AN "UNDERVALUED"

Very succinctly—the price rise could have been, and was, predictable. The alert investigator, who did a little more than hope and pray he was backing a winner, profited on the stock. A major wire house of the New York Stock Exchange recommended purchase of this stock at $10.00 per share.

This recitation of actual events raises some questions: How are these stocks located? Where are they found? How are they investigated? How can you know what is good value in a stock? Why did the stock rise? Are there definitive answers to these questions? Yes!

To apply the answers to these questions to your own investments, current and future, the following is a detailed step-by-step procedure whereby you can take available public information and evaluate the prospects of each stock held now or contemplated for purchase. There exists now—and if history is any barometer of the future, there will continue to exist—a group of securities, which, for the purpose of this book, are termed, "The Undervalueds."

BACKGROUND ON THE UNDERVALUED STOCKS

The Undervalued Stock is one which is depressed in price and affords strong asset protection to the investor while displaying very strong signs that a change for the better is taking place in the earnings outlook.

The most important element in the potential Undervalued is the change in earnings. The entire concept of making money in common stocks is predicated on the earnings performance of the corporation. By investigation and interpretation of the public information available to investors, it is possible to buy and profit from the improved performance of the corporation.

To illustrate a fairly typical Undervalued, if any such stock can be termed typical, consider for a moment the plight of the Heywood Wakefield Company during the sultry days of July 1961. The stock was selling at $13.00 per share after exerting itself to rise from a price of $9.00 a year earlier. Engaged in the highly competitive furniture field, this company had suffered the erosion of its assets through severe losses for several years.

Yet in July of 1961 this stock could have been purchased at $13.00 per share by an investor, with full knowledge that his risks of loss were minimal, and his opportunities for profit were very high. In March of 1962, or nine months later, this investor could have sold this stock at $24.00 per share.

Heywood Wakefield was not a bright star in the upper reaches of the stock market. There were no glowing reports written concerning its management, or products, or prospects. It was and is a small enterprise whose stock is traded publicly and whose price reacted in a predictable way.

Undervalued is a descriptive term applied to many kinds of stocks which have the ability and probability of increasing in price.

WHY SOME STOCKS ARE UNDERVALUED

It will be seen that Undervalued Stocks exist in every market. With so many people looking constantly for stocks with good profit potential, it will be advantageous to examine some of the reasons why the Undervalueds are overlooked and neglected.

It is a human characteristic to avoid danger. Acting on the first law of nature, the investor tries to avoid being hurt or maimed financially. It must be recognized that the Undervalueds are sometimes cripples of the stock market. Formerly healthy, some of the blue chip quality, they have fallen from grace. During their fall, they have dragged down many investors.

Put yourself in the position of the investor who paid $60.00 per share for S. H. Kress & Co. in 1946. Perhaps because of "putting them away and forgetting them," you awoke early in 1963 to see the stock selling at $18.00 per share. Envision, if you will, all of the investors over all those years who purchased the stock "on its way down," expecting a recovery, and who saw it continue its downhill ride.

Enlarge your vision to include all those who witnessed the slide—the family and friends who were apprised of the investor's grief—in short, multiply the dreaded specter of losses by all those witnesses and you have an image of why the S. H. Kress & Co. stock lacked appeal to investors.

Low Prices Are Not Accidents

The Undervalueds are undervalued for a reason. There is no dispute with a market price that is very low on a stock that has failed to earn money. Investors recognize this and steer shy of such stocks. Yet it is this very fact which provides opportunity. Just as many stocks are overenthusiastically bought and driven to unreasonably high prices, so in the other direction are some stocks overenthusiastically sold and driven down to unreasonably low prices. When many investors have been hurt by a drop in a stock, and especially when this drop has taken place over a long time, there is an emotional block against reinvesting in that stock. The fact that "losers" don't pay is exemplified in every walk of life. The defeated candidate for public office is soon forgotten. The movie star of yesteryear is the fallen star of today. The examples are plentiful but the trait is clear.

A well-known Wall Street professional was queried on the merits of the Standard Fruit and Steamship Company in the summer of 1961 when the stock was priced at 4½–5. His answer was a disdainful, "It's worth more dead than alive." Eight months later the stock was quoted 10–10½. All of us will react predictably to a situation which has proven unsuccessful in the past. However, since profit is the goal of investing, and since profits can be made in Undervalued stocks with a minimizing of risk, these stocks are well worth evaluating. Because the Undervalued stocks are overlooked—in fact disdained—by investors because of poor earnings, the prospective buyers of such issues can profit if the answer to one question can be supplied: Where does this low priced stock go from here?

Possible Consequences of Corporate Losses

Examine what the possibilities are in a low-priced stock which has been losing money. Referring again to Standard Fruit and Steamship Company—in July of 1961, when it was selling for $5.00, there were three possibilities:

1. Losses could have continued, with a consequent absorption of assets, and ultimately resulted in liquidation of the company. The result for the investor—probably total loss.

2. By earning enough to break even, the company could prolong its existence over a period of years. The result for the investor—capital tied up in a nondividend paying security; possibly no change in price of the stock; or possibly losses due to the drift downward in price occasioned by other owners of shares selling.

3. A return to strong earnings. The result to the stockholders—profit. It is

an almost inexorable law of the stock market that, given earnings and a fair prospect for their continuance and improvement, the stock will be exposed to buying pressure and consequently rise in price.

The third possibility is what we are concerned with. Given the conditions of the Undervalued—i.e., low price and lack of investor interest—the conscientious investor is presented with the challenge of determining "where will the company go from here." Based on the answer to that question, decisions will be made to discard, wait, or buy.

WHERE ARE THE UNDERVALUED STOCKS?

Because the investor is interested in profits, it often becomes necessary to put aside the all too human prejudices against investing in depressed stocks. It becomes necessary to examine every stock from the viewpoint that the sick stock or depressed industry may not always be depressed. The ability to adopt a detached view of the promise and potential of the Undervalued Stock opens the door to every conceivable type of common stock.

The stock market has two separate trading arenas: listed securities, which are those traded on exchanges by public auctions; and over-the-counter securities, which are traded by dealers who buy and sell for their own (principals) or customers' accounts (agents). The exact number of companies whose shares are traded publicly is unknown. Although we know the number of stocks listed on the New York Stock Exchange and the various regional exchanges, the over-the-counter market has estimates varying from 25,000 to 50,000 different stocks.

WHERE AMONG THESE ARE THE UNDERVALUEDS?

They are in every market and are constantly rearing their heads and begging to be purchased.

INHERENT DANGERS IN THE UNDERVALUEDS

The Undervalueds offer tremendous opportunity, but before proceeding with a study of these stocks, it might be well to mention some of their inherent dangers.

Because we are involved with depressed stocks, it is of paramount importance that every precaution be taken to preserve capital.

Many hundreds of companies fail each year. The line between survival and oblivion is often as thin as a short-term liability. The fact that a stock is low priced is in itself a danger signal. The stock market is far from being foolish and does not assign low prices to valuable stocks without a good reason. Companies have gone bankrupt and will continue to do so as long as free enterprise exists. The possibilities of further declines in earnings and stock prices must not be overlooked. The unknown and unforeseeable is always a present danger.

There is no panacea in the method of selection and evaluation described in the following chapters. But there is a great reduction in risk to be gained from intelligent application to a given stock of the meaningful facts found in this book.

Profits are probable—not guaranteed. Risk is reduced—not eliminated. The Undervalueds are present and available, but they must be located, evaluated, and judged. This will require work. It is hoped you will find the process challenging and rewarding.

2

The Importance of
Information

This section gives the kind of information needed for profitable investment in the Undervalued Stock as well as the sources available. A summary of how the professional analyst puts information to work for his clients is also covered.

Trading in stocks started under the shade of a tree on Broad Street near the Battery in downtown New York. The open auction of securities took place then much as it does today. Men who traded frequently were at the Buttonwood tree every day and began to take orders for acquaintances who traded less frequently. The growth and expansion of this practice resulted in the formulation of a voluntary association with rules and regulations binding each of the members. As time passed, trading and executing orders for the general public increased in volume, as did the numbers of stocks offered. With this growth in the number of corporations offering their securities for sale to the public, the exchange recognized its responsibilities to its customers, and began to demand certain specific information about the corporations whose stocks were traded. As this was a departure from the historic pattern of business, there were shouts and screams of "invasion of privacy."

THE WHYS OF INFORMATION

The members of the exchange and other responsible members of the financial community realized that the success of business, and its ability to raise money for growth, depended on the confidence of the public in the integrity of the corporation. It was recognized that information—accurate information—of the financial and operating performance of the corporation was the only yardstick available to the investor to measure his prospects for gain and the continuance of income. For example, stocks in the early days were purchased with much greater weight given to asset value and dividend yield than is today the case. The investor who purchased a stock paying 5 per cent annually would be badly shattered to find, six months after the purchase, that the dividend had been passed and the company was on the brink of bankruptcy. The absence of reliable information was often the cause of mistake.

The investment community, working in concert, finally persuaded the corporation to submit annual reports to their stockholders and to the exchange. This was, by no means, a cure-all of the abuses extant in the investment field, but the magnitude of the achievement can be realized when it is seen that the European business community is only now coming to realize that information is a spur and incentive for the public to invest in industry. It was because of this reporting of corporate progress that publicly held companies could come to the market for financing of new plants and processes and products over these past 60 years of fantastic growth.

As time passed and growth occurred in industry, in the number of stockholders and in the investment community, the New York Stock Exchange flexed its muscles further, and on behalf of its customers (the public) made greater demands for information on the corporations which desired to be listed on its rolls. This keystone of information was recognized as an indispensable weapon of self-defense for the investor.

The example of the American financial community succeeding in bringing American industry into the position of public-minded consciousness reflects the willingness of industry to depart from the ancient European practice of cartels and corporate secrecy by cooperating fully in advertising not only its products, but its progress, and accounts in great measure for American industrial success.

Growth in the Number of Investors

The 1929 crash in the stock market brought to the fore a subclimax to a revolutionary development that is still going on in the investment field. Prior to, and for some time following World War I, investors have been confined to a relatively small segment of the population. Merchants, traders, industrialists, and bankers who were knowledgeable and somewhat sophisticated about the whys and wherefores of business practices constituted the bulk of all investors.

Soon after World War I, the general public, through improved communications, became aware not only of the fact that America was a big country but that it was fast becoming an industrial giant.

The desire to share this growth was translated in dollars passing into stocks. Scanty information and weak corporations were no obstacle to higher prices of stocks traded during the Twenties.

The reliance on tips, rumors, and hopes, instead of on facts, resulted in a binge of spending on thin margin that left a terrible hangover through the Thirties. Voices of warning against speculation were decried as voices of doom crying out in a paradise of profit.

The walls tumbled down and the causes, in retrospect, were all too clear. Among them was the fact that emotion had trampled reason.

PRESENT STATUS OF THE SECURITIES MARKET

With the passage of the Securities Acts of 1932 and 1933, the Federal Government, using the practices of the New York Stock Exchange as a basis for legislation, set forth the requirements for the operation of stock exchanges, as well as requirements for full disclosure of all material facts by all companies using the securities market to raise money. The Security and Exchange Commission serves as the watchdog of the securities market, with the Attorney General serving as the enforcement arm of the Government.

It is evident that the actions taken by the financial community (and by the Congress in legislation) to safeguard the investors' interest has been done by requiring the disclosure of information to the public.

The present-day status of industry, stock exchanges, and the investing public is one where the public is given a tremendous amount of data by industry. The exchange, through its member firms, disseminates and often interprets the information, and the public falls back on these judgments to make its dollars-and-cents decision.

INFORMATION AS THE BASIS FOR INVESTMENT DECISIONS

The importance of information to the investor cannot be minimized—"inside" information, not rumors, but facts relating to the strength, size, stability, health, and goals of the corporation are the keys to success in investing. The dissemination of information of all types is now so widespread that we take it for granted, and, like so many things taken for granted, we frequently do not use it.

It is the information about corporations which concerns us throughout these pages. The types of information available, where it is found, the form it takes, the terms used to present that information, the meaning, the interpretations and the conclusions to be drawn from the facts, form a large part of this system of the Undervalueds.

THE CORPORATE REPORTS

The greatest single source of meaningful information to the investor is the financial report of the corporation. Of these reports, the year-end statements (annual reports) are the most comprehensive. The modern-day annual report contains a great deal of information about plants, products, goals, and performance, but the most important items are the balance sheet (what the company owns and what it owes) and the income or operating statement (what monies came in during the year and where they were spent). The annual report for many companies is the only report rendered to the stockholders. Small companies with a desire for anonymity, coupled with a distaste for the expense of preparing interim reports, often make only one report. The companies' stockholders are left dangling over a foggy bottom from year to year, and significant changes of any kind are hidden by omission for twelve months.

The Danger of Inadequate Information

It is a serious hazard to risk substantial losses in marginal companies because there is insufficient information available to enable the investor to make a decision. Consider the case of an owner of 100 shares of X Company. Assume the stock was purchased at a price of $8.00 per share on the basis of earnings of 79¢ per share for the year 1959. Purchased in March of 1960, when the annual report was made, this investor watched the stock rise to a price of $10.00 within two months, and then start to drift down to $9.00, then to his purchase price of $8.00. At this point, he frets somewhat but assumes it is just "the vagaries of the market." At a price of $6.00 he is worried, and the decision to sell and accept a loss of 25 per cent of his investment gnaws and tugs with the conflicting hope that the price will "turn around" and return to $8.00 at which point he vows he will sell. Having decided that no decision is the best decision—generally, too, it is the easiest and most often the wrong one—this investor now tries—to no avail—to get some information about the company's current status of sales and earnings. He is in the awkward position of having nothing on which to base a logical decision. When the stock is at $4 nine months after his purchase, he is still in the dark as to what is happening and is faced with the prospect of loss of 50 per cent of his investment. He throws up his hands and says he will "wait it out."

The end of the year brings another annual report and it would be logical to expect that performance has not been good. Such is the case, since the figures show the X Company has gone into the red, showing a deficit of .08¢ per share.

The shareholder was operating with a blindfold. With quarterly or even semi-annual reports, the trend in earnings would probably have been discernible and intelligent action could have been taken based on available facts.

The drifting downward of the stock price during the year was occasioned by the leakage of facts about sales and earnings through directors, officers, and suppliers of the company, as well as customers of the firm. This is an inescapable fact of economic life. There is anticipation of bad as well as good results. Stocks move in price for a reason. It is therefore imperative that the investor use all available information about the company's performance and prospects to help him make decisions.

In this study of Undervalued Stocks, our primary concern is with corporate information. This is the step which enables us to climb toward profits. It is not only the source, however, but the collection and dissemination of this information which concerns the prospective investor.

ADVANTAGE OF A LISTED SECURITY

Information requirements of listed companies are more stringent than unlisted or over-the-counter stocks.

The company whose stock is listed on the New York Stock Exchange is required to submit to stockholders and to the Exchange annual and interim reports of its financial condition. These reports show sales, earnings (or losses) on a per share and in total dollar amounts, operating expenses or costs, and in a brief way tell the shareholder what, and how well, his company is doing.

By this means, the shareholder is able to maintain a current or reasonably current picture of his company's direction, and thereby make "sell" or "buy" decisions based on performance.

In addition to the formal reports about financial condition, management will, during the course of the year, announce to the press and the stockholders newsworthy items of any changes that are about to, or have taken place, in markets, products, plants, management, new financings, acquisitions, etc.

This is the information which generations of men have fought to obtain for stockholders: the news of performance facts which can, or might, affect the prices of the shares in the market. This is the information which permits you to examine, evaluate, and measure your prospects for profit through equity investment. This is the information about listed companies which is so often neglected, overlooked, and ignored to the financial detriment of the investor.

THE UNLISTED SECURITY

What about the unlisted security, the over-the-counter stock? Herein lies a problem. There are some of America's largest companies whose shares are traded "over the counter": Traveler's Insurance Co. (with a few exceptions all insurance stocks are traded there); Time, Inc.; Avon Products; and almost all bank stocks. But some of America's smallest and most obscure companies trade here also. Some companies publish interim reports as well as annual ones. Because these companies are not on a regulated exchange, they may exercise their own option whether to comply with minimum requirements of the Securities Act, and publish just one report annually, or, on their own volition, report quarterly. It therefore becomes essential for the prudent investor to look before he leaps, to see how often and whether the company will leave him in darkness for a year or six months. In other words, risks increase in proportion to a decrease in available information.

Since we will be concerning ourselves with the balance sheet, the income statement, and the quarterly reports, it will be important to determine where we can find them.

THE FINANCIAL SERVICES

Let us assume that a business acquaintance whose judgment you respect suggested in the summer of 1961 that you purchase some shares in the Conrad Carson Company. Upon calling your broker, you found that the price was $6.00 per share. His opinion was: "I've never heard of the company, but if you are interested I will investigate it for you." You agree with this suggestion and request that he call you.

The broker avails himself of one of several financial reporting services. He locates Conrad Carson and finds a very brief summary report on the company's 1959 year-end condition. Earnings show a loss, the company is a newcomer to the field, and its general financial condition is weak (net current assets of $310). Based on the gathering of these scant facts, the broker calls you and advises that though there is no current information available on the company's outlook, or management, or new products, and based on the weakness shown in the previous year-end statement, the investment is extremely speculative and could only be characterized as a gamble.

The important part here is not the recommendation but the availability of some information. Recognizing that we are dealing with a tiny company operating on a local (California) level, it is obvious that the sole hope of making any kind of decision rests on up-to-date information.

Although all information originates with the corporation, our interest lies in where we can obtain it without resorting to extensive correspondence with the company or to other time-consuming devices.

The financial reporting services are the easiest and most complete sources of corporate news and financial reports. For the purposes of the Undervalued Stocks, we have used Standard & Poor's Monthly Stock Guide for the first step in the examination process, and Moody's Industrials for the subsequent steps. It is not suggested that these volumes necessarily become a part of your library, but the monthly Stock Guide should be accessible and the large volumes of Moody's and Standard & Poor's are, or should be, as close as your public library.

Type of Coverage Offered

The amount of information compiled within the covers of these annual volumes is staggering: announcements of mergers, acquisitions, new financings, management changes. Anything and everything of any consequence affecting thousands of corporations, large and small, is collected by these major services. The quarterly reports and annual reports, as well as brief descriptive histories of the companies and their products, are included.

The tool used to unlock the doors to sound investing is information. Standard & Poor's, Moody's, and Fitch's are the leading services. (Please note that we are dealing here only with industrials. Each of the services, with some variations, provides equivalent information on transportation—rails primarily—utilities, and bank stocks; insurance companies are in a class of their own and "Best's" is the recognized source of information on these companies.) It is essential that the investor have available in the local library one or all three of these services.

(The previous example of the Conrad Carson Company showed that stock to have been selling at $6.00 per share in the summer of 1961. The casual investor who heeded the advice to invest could have sold his shares in December 1961 for $1.00 per share, or a whopping 83.3 per cent loss of capital.)

The Undervalued method of stock investing takes elemental, available information and permits—in fact, demands—that definite conclusion be drawn from these facts.

In three stages, each growing progressively deeper and broader, a company that has engaged our attention through a public announcement is subjected to a limited but meaningful examination of its underpinnings.

The fact that this system of investigation is limited does not detract from its merits. Covering only the financial bones and sinews of the corporation under study, we accept the limitations of time, money, and geography that prevent our fleshing out the entire body of the corporation structure.

THE PROFESSIONAL ANALYSIS

It is the bone and sinew which we shall seek, but to understand the contrast with a full-scale professional analysis, it may be well to examine what many brokerage firms offer as a free service to their customers.

The research director of a large securities firm receives a report in July 1961 from the senior analyst in charge of the heavy machinery industry that the E. W. Bliss Company appears to be making significant progress in earnings. He also notes that recent Government actions of increasing depreciation allowances on capital goods adds some interest to these stocks. The research director, basing his decision on up-to-date information on Government policies, economic trends, industrial and consumer spending outlook, agrees with his senior analyst's suggestions and asks for some details on this particular company in this particular industry. The senior analyst has a report prepared by one of his assistants showing the current "bone and sinew" of E. W. Bliss: meaningful facts such as sales, sales trend, profit margins, earnings, dividends, and asset values; an abbreviated picture of the health of the subject.

Statistical Analysis

If the initial report passes its tests, instructions are issued to "make a study" of this unsuspecting company. One or possibly two men are assigned to make up a comprehensive financial analysis of E. W. Bliss, covering a period of time as far back as 10 years. Annual reports are examined closely for product information and progress reports on new developments. Research expenditures are weighed and compared with those of other companies. Management changes and acquisitions are noted, and the financial structure is broken down and weighed in the fatal scale of safety and value. When all available facts are assembled in meaningful order, a second phase is carried out—comparison.

E. W. Bliss is now measured against its competitions within the industry. How has it performed in earnings, sales, profit margins, market penetration, costs, research, and new products, compared to other firms in the same industry?

This study is now reviewed by the senior analyst who is in charge of the heavy machinery industry. It is reviewed objectively, without personal involvement, for or against investing. The strengths and weaknesses that have appeared in this still embryonic stage of investigation are measured.

With or without comments from the senior analyst, the report is submitted to the director of research. Perhaps two weeks have passed and two men have devoted their own special talents plus eight hours a day to uncovering the facts needed for a further judgment to be made.

Field Trips

With this report, the director of research is now in a position to decide whether E. W. Bliss looks strong enough to warrant further investigation. In this case, the decision is made that it is. The senior analyst is requested to make arrangements to visit the company. This is the final phase of the analysis. An experienced analyst visits the plants and offices of the company. He is armed with voluminous information about what has happened in the past. The purpose of the field trip is to analyze management (which, after all, is the driving force behind the company), and, most importantly, to determine the potential of the company.

The image of a brash young man asking inane questions of busy executives is far from the actual case. Realizing the restrictions imposed on management from revealing "inside" information, and the limitations on what and how much can be told of future plans and products, the analyst must operate within the confines of the business and moral ethic to reach valid conclusions based on seemingly disconnected facts. For example, let us suppose that the 10-year history of a company had shown that management was constantly forecasting sales through its inventories. To illustrate, assume that year-end inventories were invariably one-twelfth to one-eleventh of the first six months sales of the succeeding year. Our well-armed analyst might very well find out the current inventory figures and achieve a reasonable sales forecast of his own. This fact, coupled with sales projections and backlog of orders on hand supplied by management, may enable the analyst to reach a valid conclusion of "projected" earnings for the period under consideration. If the company has shown a stable percentage of net profit on sales over the previous five to eight years, and if there are currently no adverse factors in sight to affect this profit percentage, the analyst will be able to compute the projected earnings as a percentage of projected sales based on orders, sales, and backlog reinforced by the inventory ratio.

During the interviews, a good deal of time is spent on questions relating to competition, new markets or new merchandising methods. The treasurer is interviewed to obtain information on whether new capital will be needed to carry out planned expansions, and, if this is the case, how much and of what type. The plant manager or production chief may be a source of information about improved operating procedures or inefficiencies.

With a full notebook, not the least part of which contains pertinent comments on management (attitudes, aggressiveness, competence, reliability, secretiveness, cooperativeness, age, goals, morale) the analyst heads for the home office, which may be an hour's drive or a day's airplane flight away, to compile his report.

In the case of E. W. Bliss, a report is submitted to the research director, outlining the facts and conclusions of the analyst. After reading it, the director confers with his analyst to obtain those invaluable unwordable impressions of the company and its people.

The Final Test

Having withstood the test of fundamentals, the final test is the market. A recommendation to buy E. W. Bliss is incorporated in a printed report that summarizes the findings of the research staff. The report is reviewed by responsible officers of the firm and distributed to all the registered representatives. From these men comes the exercise of further judgment: Is this a good investment for my accounts? Experience in the market, a knowledge of stock price movements, an intimate knowledge of the needs and aims of his own accounts will determine whether the E. W. Bliss report is submitted to you—the final judge and jury of the merits of a particular issue at a particular time at a particular price.

This description of what a good investment firm will do in order to achieve success for itself, through the success of its clients, is an illustration of two facts: first, that there are, cost-free, gold mines of information available through reputable investment firms; and secondly, given the method of the Undervalueds, your ability to render judgment on reports so obtained will be mightily enhanced.

3

The Problems
Common to
All Investors

The three major problems involved in investing in common stocks are reviewed within the framework of the market. The confrontations and solution of these problems through the Undervalued Stock is treated in some detail.

Liberty Fabrics is a small company whose stock is traded on the American Stock Exchange. During the late winter and spring of 1962, this stock almost doubled in price while the rest of the market was experiencing a substantial sell-off.

An examination of this price movement and the problems faced by investors at all price levels may help to illustrate the problems constantly besieging the "successful" investor.

In February of 1962, Liberty Fabrics announced that its earnings for fiscal 1961 were $1.00 per share. The stock was selling at $22.00. At this price, it was at a rather "rich" level during a market period when most stocks were going down. Twenty-two times earnings is not inexpensive for a small, relatively untried corporation. Neglecting for the moment the yardstick for measuring value, assume that you were incited to buy Liberty Fabrics stock at this price at that time. Because information is your cornerstone for successful investing, you asked, "Why should I purchase this stock?" and the advisor informed you as follows:

"Liberty Fabrics has just announced their full year earnings of $1.00 per share. It is evident that this stock is not cheap at this price. In fact, it is at its highest price, but it does represent a very promising 'speculation.' This public corporation has been marketing a new product, which is a molded brassiere. Sales have increased substantially and market acceptance looks very promising. There is a good possibility that they will earn between $2.00 and $3.00 a share this year (1962). The reason it is speculative is because of the possibility that other firms will enter competing products. Marketing and sales are purely estimates at this time and general stock market conditions are shaky."

THE PURCHASE PROBLEM

Without subjecting ourselves to more detailed analysis of this stock, let us assume that you purchased the stock. With more than some misgivings, you ordered the purchase of 100 shares. Now the die was cast. Within four days, your $2,200 had to be paid. Perhaps that evening you heard the market report and the averages were down. The seed of doubt that was planted as soon as you ordered the stock is now a pang of fear that you have made a bad blunder. The reason for the fear is the speculative nature of the stock, the fact that you have bought at the "high" and the added weight of fear occasioned by the market's poor performance. After snarling at your wife and children, resignation sets in as you bury your fear in the knowledge that no decision can be made that night and you "forget it." (The stock closed down one-half point from your purchase price.)

Here is exemplified the first of the three separate but united problems faced by all investors in all markets at all times. This first problem is the "timing of the purchase."

Once you have committed yourself to a stock, you have solved for better or worse two problems: selection and timing. Selection, as we shall see, will have been solved through information and investigation, but "timing" now puts you into active competition with all other buyers and sellers in that stock. Now you are in, and judgment has decided the course. You could have delayed the decision (as so many do) by telling your broker to "wait for a lower price," or, "Let's see what happens in the next few days." These are no more than reflections of indecision, not necessarily on whether to invest, but more pointedly *when* to invest.

Imagine the doubts of the investor who paid $115 per share for Beckman Instruments. How high is high? Is 50 times earnings too high a price? Usually it is plain rashness that would move an investor into a stock at that high a level, but there are enough exceptions to the rule to render this, like most generalizations, incorrect.

The normal doubts inherent in all speculative investments continue as within the next few weeks Liberty Fabrics vacillates between 21 and 24; but a certain assurance comes from the fact that your stock seems immune to general market performance. (No decision needed or made during this period.)

A month later, your children are wide-eyed as, at the end of another day, you discharge expensive gifts all over the kitchen table on your arrival home. Your wife eyes this unaccustomed generosity with more than a little suspicion until informed that your broker called to tell you that the Liberty Fabrics closed at a price of $26.00. Four hundred dollars, or a paper profit of almost 25 per cent (these percentages of gain are always overstated, while percentages of loss are invariably understated), serves to allay your wife's suspicions and all is serene in Mr. Investor's household.

The following day, the stock climbs 3 points to 29, and ebullient joy is replaced with sober satisfaction at the astuteness you displayed in shrewdly selecting this stock. You walk straighter, and there is a new note of confidence and authority in your voice. The next day the stock holds at the 29 level and the following day it slides back to 26. Your broker calls (this one calls with bad news as well as good) and advises that you wait—there is a possibility that all of your gains will be wiped out but an equal chance that the stock will rebound. Succumbing to this advice, an unpleasant evening is spent in which firm mental kicks are implanted for failing to sell at $29.00. The $300 paper profit lost that day is counted against all the things it would have provided for your family. To no avail—recrimination has no merit except as a lesson for the future. With this thought, you determine to sell the next day, no matter what. This stock has acted like a yo-yo—up three, down three. Why not down another three tomorrow?

The broker advises that, because this is a volatile stock with a high degree of speculativeness, he cannot accord any reasons strong enough to deter you from selling. So the stock is sold, and more by chance than design you obtain a price of $28.00 on the sale. It was on its way back up.

Satisfied with a $600 profit (less commissions and within a year less a short-term capital gains tax), you watch the stock move to a high of $39.00 per share and then commence a drift downward. A twinge of regret possesses you briefly as this event is noted, but, like all intelligent investors, you rest content on a profit realized and give short shrift to "what might have been" and take solace from the truism, "No one ever went broke taking profits."

DISCOUNTING

Most important in this investment situation is the problem faced by you as the investor when the stock went up in price. What had happened to cause its rise, and what had happened to cause you to sell?

The reason for the abrupt price movement of the stock was that the market (investors) were *discounting* the anticipated earnings increase by Liberty Fabrics.

The dictionary defines discounting as "a deduction from an original price or debt allowed for paying promptly or in cash."

The meaning of "discounting" in the parlance of the stock market is the buying or selling of securities in anticipation of an event or occurrence which may or will affect the earnings of a company some time in the future.

Discounting on the Way Down

For example, in 1962, during a boom year for automobile sales, Chrysler Corporation lost a good portion of the sales market to its competitors. The 1961 earnings for the corporation were quite thin. Did the stock go down during the early months of that year when prices were tumbling all over the market place? No! Chrysler went up in price because investors were anticipating (discounting) the good news of cost cutting, new management, a new turbine engine, and a newly styled line of cars promised for the 1963 model. This anticipated improvement was realized as earnings for 1962 amounting to $5.37 versus $1.24 for the previous year.

Discounting is anticipating everything and anything which might affect particular issues of particular times.

Discounting is the *single greatest* problem faced in all markets at all times. It is the problem which overlaps and affects the problems of timing the sale and the purchase of securities.

Discounting is the double-dealing Jezebel which causes the stock you just purchased to plummet down the next day. It is the whey-faced imp which causes the stock you just sold to go up 10 points within two weeks of your sale.

Discounting is a black-hearted scoundrel when your stocks are dropping and a blood-tingling siren when your stocks are reaching for the sky.

This element, which the market calls discounting, is the spice, verve, and risk of investing that constitutes the challenge and the promise of the free market. It is nothing more than the weight—the constantly shifting weight—of buyers and sellers exercising their judgment on the merits or demerits of a particular stock. The action in price of a stock is the best indication of how discounting works.

Discounting on the Way Up

Polaroid Corporation, the manufacturer of the famous Land camera, was selling at a price as high as $261 per share in late 1961. The company was indicating earnings for the full year at slightly more than those achieved in 1960 ($2.07 for 1961 vs. $2.06 for 1960). The price of the stock started drifting down until it hit $220, or approximately 105 times earnings. It managed to waver around this price, dipping and weaving as much as 50 points on a cycle through a down market, buoyed in price by investors' hopes for the success of a new color film for the camera.

Reluctant to sell because of hopes for the future, most shareholders watched as some of the realists sold their shares. With few courageous buyers available, the price dropped. Slowly but inexorably, the price slid beneath 200.

Fear of future losses (anticipations) served to shake loose hopes for gain, and the selling increased. On May 12, 1962, a selling crescendo had built up as sellers crowded and elbowed their way to the trading post and sent Polariod down 23 points to a price of $143. In June, it dropped further to $81.00. This was a reaction to overdiscounting. The price of the stock had been overenthusiastically carried to a point where years would elapse before the company could possibly earn an amount that would warrant such a high price on this stock. The emotional pitch of sustained and substantial advances in price had blinded many successful investors to the possibility that the price could come down much more quickly than it rose.

Discounting Both Ways

Discounting is a two-way street. The good news is often anticipated by rumor months before the event and stocks rise on the rumored good news. When the news becomes fact, many holders sell on the news and bewilder the layman, who sees a drop in price of the stock. For example, Ford announced that its directors had submitted a proposal for a two-for-one stock split to its shareholders. The stock dipped three points on the news. Why? Because rumors of an impending split had been rife for some months. The stock had gone from a price of $80 to a high of $116 over a period of several months. When the news was announced, there was a reaction in price, because speculators knew there would be no more discounting for a while and because there was some disappointment that the split was not three-for-one.

THE QUESTION OF TAKING PROFITS

To revert to the original example, the discounting of earnings (possible earnings) of $2.00 to $3.00 per share for Liberty Fabrics sent the price to a high of $39.00. This rise was abrupt but not in a straight line. The stock at $39.00 was selling at a high multiple of 1961 earnings (39 times) but a reasonable 15½ times projected earnings of $2.50 per share. Now the investor who still held the stock is indeed in a quandary (a very pleasant quandary, however). "Shall I sell and take a short-term profit, or sit tight and at least wait for the six-months period?" Will it drop in price as fast as it went up? Maybe if they make $3.00 per share it can sell at 20 times earnings ($60.00 per share), and who knows what I should do? The perennial dilemma is posed: when to sell? This is the third problem: the timing of the sale.

TIMING THE SALE

How many investors have lived through the harrowing experience of see-ing sizeable gains evaporate into losses as they sit hypnotized by the previous gains and keep wishing and hoping for the return or turn around in price. With wishes and hopes contributing to investor myopia, purses are often lighter by sizeable sums. If the market is strong, running at a high level of volume, and generally higher in the market indicators, many owners of stocks of doubtful merit will tend to retain their ownership in the hope that general enthusiasm will raise prices. The reverse sentiment is evidenced in down markets, when questionable stocks are held with the rationale that "it is foolish to sell at a loss." The decision to sell at a loss is an anguished one—delayed by hopes for a turn and put out of mind for as long as possible. Finally faced when all hope runs out, the losses are generally much larger than would have been necessary.

Concerning the sale of stocks that have risen in value, greed often over-comes reason. The investor who purchased Vendo Corporation at $44.00 and saw it continue animatedly upward to $77.00 is doubtless quite uncomfortable with the thought of "what might have been" had he sold in the high fifties or sixties. This stock dribbled down in price to the mid-twenties. Regrets over paper profits that are now paper losses are part of the personal portfolio of every investor.

Having examined the three problems of timing—the purchase, discounting, and selling—we shall examine these problems in the light of the Undervalued stock.

THE UNDERVALUED STOCK AND THE INVESTORS' PROBLEMS

Because the Undervalueds are the neglected issues in the market, they enjoy certain unique advantages. The first advantage is that they are selling at or near their historic lows in price, or they are selling at an extremely low price in relation to earnings.

The psychology of the stock market is an almost perfect mirror of human nature. This is a great part of the fascination and challenge of the market, as well as an inevitable result, since people make the market.

DISCOUNTING AND THE UNDERVALUED STOCK

The shareowner who purchases a stock that has been zooming up in price is constantly beset by doubts and fears of an equally fast decline. In the realm of the Undervalueds, the aura of success has been burnished off the neglected failures. There are no enthusiastic fluctuations in price as sentiment sways purchases and sales. The Undervalueds are the poor relatives of the market, shunted into the shade to eke out their miserable price levels. Sad as this may seem, this condition offers a bright prospect to the investor. He is able to examine his potential selection in the unclouded valleys of the market without the mist and high velocity winds which buffet the glamour issues high on the crest. The Undervalueds which are giving off unmistakable signs of strong ✓ recovery can be purchased at a low price in a calculated, unemotional, precise fashion, based on fact. Because of the clarity of vision afforded by these stocks, the investor is handed another advantage with which to work for profit.

The solution to the problem of discounting is never 100 per cent complete. Because the investor is an inveterate optimist, discounting is never completely eliminated, but it is reduced to nominal proportions in the Undervalued stocks.

TIMING THE SALE OF THE UNDERVALUED

Many investors with shrewd judgment neatly solve the problems of timing the purchase but flounder completely with the timing of sale. It is again a human trait that "success begets success," and the investor who sees substantial gains in price from his purchase level very often becomes surprised when the course reverses. It is also true that many brokers will recommend purchase levels and fall prey to the same failing of neglecting "sell" recommendations. The reasons for this situation vary with each stock, but essentially the problem lies in determining when the discounting of future performance becomes so great that vulnerability to losses exceeds possible further gains. The only reason for sale is faltering performance or reversal of performance by the company. It is not enough to purchase a stock based on sound information, intelligently interpreted, and then forget the company and think only in terms of "the market." Stock prices move for a reason. That reason reverts in the final analysis to the company's performance. The great losers in the investment arena are those who sell with small profits and large losses. The investor who sees a small profit and immediately seizes it *"because it is a profit"* is doing himself great damage. He probably has devoted considerable effort to selecting, investigating, and investing, using judgment based on reason, and then defeats his efforts by succumbing to the temptation of realized gains before the stock has a chance to prove itself. The sale, like the purchase, must be based on facts or based on the stock, reaching a price so far out of proportion to future as well as present performance that it becomes dangerously liable to substantial decline.

Selling on Performance

Examine the first reason for sale—the performance of the company. Assume that Beech-Nut Life Savers had been purchased at a price of $41.00 per share in 1960. The stock reached a high of $88.00 per share in 1961 and then drifted somewhat aimlessly through the early months of the "Kennedy Bear Market" of 1962 down to a price of $70.00. Do you sell? No. The company's earnings, marketing, management, and new products have shown unmistakable signs of continuing their previous good performance. There was no fundamental reason to sell this stock at that time. There was a fair market valuation in relation to earnings and prospects for continued improvement in value. Contrast this to General Instruments Corporation. Assume purchase at $27.00 in 1960 and a rise in price to $53.00 the following year. The electronics boom was showing unmistakable signs of weakening as competition, obsolescence, and generally crowded conditions cut back on the glamour of growth. Earnings showed a decline, as did sales. Profit margins were reduced. Every fundamental fact pointed to a sale, including the high price to earnings ratio of the stock. There were ample indications to sell, and those who followed facts, not hopes, did sell. They sold the stock down to price below $20.00 in a matter of months.

Regarding the Undervalueds, it is necessary to continue to watch the stock—not just the price, but the company's performance. If, for example, Standard Fruit and Steamship was purchased at a price of $6.00 in early 1962 and the price was $12.00 in May of the same year, the stock would *not* be sold. The price rose for a reason, and the reason was a dramatic return to profitable operations. As long as the *rate* of profitability remains constant or improves, the stock will be retained until the price reaches a level consonant with its earnings. In retrospect, it is always easy to see what should have been, but with stock held now your only weapon is knowledge. If a corporation earns, in its first quarter, $1.20 per share, and the stock is selling at $12.00, that stock is still Undervalued in relation to annual earnings. If the second-quarter earnings show a maintenance or improvement of this rate, it will be wise to hold the stock further. If the third-quarter report shows a decline in earnings, sales, or profit margins, the sell signal will have appeared. There is no known method of being able to sell at the high. There is a method of calculating when to sell based on reason and fact.

Selling on Price and Judgment

The second reason for selling is more difficult because it is emotional in nature. If a stock has run up very sharply in price, such as Liberty Fabrics from $22.00 to $39.00 in a three-month period, the investor must look at the size of his profit, the quality of the company, and the psychology of the market. His profits are very high, 80 per cent in gains, the company is small and untried, the product has promise, but for the here and now the market has pretty substantially discounted the good news. The market in general at that time was bearish—i.e., selling pressures had been quite heavy for some months.

Prudence would dictate sale when the stock started to drift back in price. The considerations used are primarily the application of common-sense judgment. In each situation, different factors will affect your judgment. The close attention to financial and performance reports of the company is the safest yardstick to use for decisions, and in the case of the Undervalued stock this is the criterion that has been used.

The use of the Undervalued stock for investing for profit is not an exercise in buying "losers." There are present, in all markets, stocks which have been neglected, which give off strong signals of meaningful change. The ability to recognize the opportunities, as well as the knowledge to interpret the facts, is all that is necessary to arm you for your assault on the market.

The seemingly simple disposal of the problems of timing and discounting as applied to Undervalued Stocks is not a mirage, nor is it a guarantee. The misreading of facts or surprise developments within an industry of the company under investigation may well throw our projections out of kilter. However, it is absolutely necessary that investigation—intelligent investigation—precede investing.

SUMMARY

The timing problems are never solved by indecision. In most cases, "sell" signals as well as "buy" signals are quite clear. Any attempt to buy at the "low" is usually expensive. The certainty of predicting a stock's fluctuations over the near term period is impossible. This is not to say that purchases are made indiscriminately, but it is to say that once the decision is made to buy, then act on the decision without trying to outguess the market. The owner of shares who is faced with a loss if he sells is very often deluding himself with hopes of recovery. The facts of earnings, profit margins, shrinking markets, declining sales, are all shunted from his mind as the rationalizations take over. Some investors speak of their losing stock with the emotion usually associated with a slur on one's wife. A veritable tirade of praise for the virtue of the company's products, the integrity of management and previous successes of the company are cited to produce more reasons for riding out the storm. Although all investors are optimists, the successful investors are realists. When changes occur that adversely affect present or future success of the company, then sell. Even if it's only one week after purchase of the stock and new information is released which is not favorable, do not be blinded by the shining newness of your purchase. Sell. The loss then will probably be smaller than three months later.

Making Profits Requires Efforts

The development of all investment is a demanding process. The institutional investors employ large staffs of competent analysts to provide as high a margin of safety as possible in conjunction with the greatest profit potential.

The individual investor has available mountains of information (at no cost in most instances) from his member firm of the New York Stock Exchange. This information will become much more valuable when intelligent judgment is superimposed on these facts.

Put the Problems to Work for You

The problems outlined here are not deterrents to investments. On the contrary, when a stock has been purchased it becomes the earnest hope that "discounting" of the particular stock purchased will be carried on by later purchasers.

The element of discounting is the single greatest profit factor in equity investment. The ability to get this "problem" to work for you is the final ability to make money from your stocks.

The selling problem is one that in most instances is simplified by performance. There are stocks that are extremely difficult to evaluate for sale. To illustrate: Revlon (the cosmetics manufacturer) was selling at a price of $81.00 in late 1961. The stock had been a highly profitable investment for some years. The price curve had been consistently upward. The owners' shares had been blessed with two stock splits in a relatively short time, but in 1961, at $81.00, the shares were selling at more than 40 times earnings, but rate of growth in earnings was slow. The problem of holding or selling was complicated by the fact of potentially high profit new product ("Eterna 27" an anti-wrinkle cosmetic), plus a history of successful merchandising of existing products. Would the promise of a new product overcome the fundamental change in growth in earnings? Reality overcame hopes. Revlon hovered in the high seventies and mid-eighties for some time and, as selling continued, it started to drift. The investor who held on watched it drop to fifty by mid-May 1962, and then into the low thirties by fall. A sale at $60.00? A sale at $52.00? Discounting works both ways. The prudent investor, who must sit out on a limb with a stock whose value is so high in relation to earnings, must be always conscious of his vulnerability to substantial declines. When this vulnerability exists, the safest course is to pocket profits or cut losses. When serious doubts exist, it is the course of the prudent man to take the doubtful stock out of his portfolio.

The Undervalued stock puts the investor in the enviable position of being able to time his purchase at or near the level where the stock is about to or has demonstrated the meaningful change in performance.

Because you have acted on facts and purchased at a price which allows substantial room for further improvement in price, it is now not only possible but probable that discounting will be working for you and not against you.

The retention of the stock is predicated on the continued good performance of the company. Any significant changes in the performance data indicating a slow-down or reversal of trend is a tangible sell signal.

4

Why Stock Prices Move

A broad review of the surface forces acting on the "market" leads to a review of the fundamental reasons which cause prices of individual issues to move. The reinforcement of these "fundamentals" as yardsticks for profits is performed through illustration.

There are two legs needed for increases in stock prices. The first leg is improved earnings. The second is an increase in the "multiplier." Either element operating alone will, in most instances, result in gains in price; but when the two elements are working together, substantial profits can be realized.

Since it is the basic aim of all investors to secure profits, it will be advantageous to examine the pricing structure of common stocks and the "solutions" used by many investors to secure these profits. The merits of the Undervalueds will be apparent when the contrasting methods are seen.

In the pre-World War I era, investors evaluated securities on the basis of a company's asset value and dividend yield. It was felt that, since the stock represented an equity interest in the assets, this was the only safe yardstick of evaluation. Following World War I and through the present time, stock prices are, ultimately, based on a company's earnings.

THE FINAL MEASURE OF VALUE-EARNINGS

The concept of earnings as a measure of value came about through the realization that, although assets were needed, the final goal of business and investors was profits. This measure of value was and is a far more accurate index of success than any other, because it provides a constant rule for all investors to use in assaying proposed and actual investments.

Because profit of some kind has been the prime motivation force for all mankind since the beginning of time, it is somehow incomprehensible how and why otherwise intelligent people have been and are attacking not only profit, but the profit motive in this country.

Contrast in Valuation

The introduction of earnings as the arbiter of stock values opened tremendous fluctuations in stock prices, as the emotional buying of large groups

49

of investors in a limited number of companies sent some stocks to high ratios of price to earnings. The old-time valuations of 10 times annual earnings (based on the businessman's view that any investment should be returned in 10 years) gave way to wild enthusiasm since the end of World War II.

Using the Dow Jones Industrial Average (30 representative stocks), these issues were selling at an average of six (6) times earnings in 1949, but in 1961 they were selling at an average of twenty-three (23) times annual earnings.

The single greatest area of confusion in common stocks is the earnings "multiplier."

Lack of Continuity of Earnings

Republic Aviation Corporation was projecting earnings of $7.00 per share in late 1961. The stock was selling in the mid-forties, or at a price less than seven times its annual earnings for that year. A buy at this bargain price of $49.00? No. The market was evaluating the stock downward (it went below $20.00 a share in 1962) because its main source of revenue, the F105D fighter plane was being phased out of production, and there were no replacement products to fill the gap in sales and earnings. The net result was a sell-off of the stock *because* there were no *promises* of future earnings. (Republic Aviation is a cyclical stock because of heavy dependence on Government contracts.)

It is therefore not only earnings but the continuation of those earnings, and in fact improvement of them, which are the criteria for high, low, and medium multipliers.

The dull, consistently static earnings corporation will not be accorded a valuation even close to the glamour favorites.

The Problems of Earnings Growth

The reason for the price performance in a stock is earnings and growth in earnings.

By retracing some of the stock market leaders, it will be noted that each year seems to bring out a new crop of "glamour" stocks.

In the early Fifties, the television stocks rocketed across the stock ticker as though television was the only worthwhile investment in the whole market. Prices were bid to fantastic heights on these issues.

During all of the excitement, RCA, or "Radio" as it is affectionately called, was marching along at $12.00 per share.

Many sober investors looked, and looked again, and bought. In a flying market, they reasoned, here was a well-seasoned blue chip selling at an extremely low price.

The predictable happened. RCA was "discovered" and it followed its television relatives across the tape in great strides upward.

Soon the same thing happened with business machine companies. Then the space age dawned and electronics pyramided tiny companies into the ether of the stock market clouds. Listed stocks, new issues (names changed on sedate little companies to give them glamour)—all of these took off in price with a feverish rise, as long as they were in the magic field of electronics.

The New York Stock Exchange saw fit to issue warnings against haphazard investment in unknown companies in unknown fields—to no avail. The race continued—40, 50, 100 times earnings and often 100 times losses; it did not seem to matter.

There was very little that could be done about when to buy, what to buy, or when to sell. Each investor was outguessing the next, and the investments were profitable or unprofitable more by chance than design.

After the sheen wore off the electronics, new areas were invaded by investors—of all things, the long, low-priced supermarket food chains. These narrow profit margin giants, which had helped in making this the best-fed nation in the world, were suddenly "glamourized." The buying of shares in Grand Union, Safeway, National Stores, Winn Dixie—it all became a matter of course. The multipliers jumped from 10 to 20 to 25.

Soon a burgeoning new industry grabbed the spotlight—discount stores—and the whole process was repeated. Korvette purchased at $22 and sold at $58 or $60 by many prudent investors went on to confound them and everyone else by rising to $120 per share and then splitting three-for-one.

It is the *hope* of every investor that he will be in stocks before the market glamourizes them and doubles or triples its historic multiplier. But this must be accorded its proper perspective: it is a hope.

WHY PRICES OF STOCKS "MOVE"

Because it is so vital to successful investing, an examination of why stock prices move goes a long way to helping make investment decisions. Think, if you will, of the dilemma of the specialist dealing in Honolulu Oil in late 1961. Since the specialist is responsible for keeping the market orderly, look at his problem as rumors are confirmed that the company has agreed to sell its assets to another company. Since the assets are valued at $103 per share, it is readily apparent that the stock is a "sure profit" selling at $84.00. Suddenly the specialist is overwhelmed with a crowd of brokers trying to buy shares. The price moves up to $92.00 very quickly, and then stampeding across the floor comes a herd of people with sell orders (it seems the Government had just obtained an injunction restraining the sale of assets and the news had just broken). Sell orders were shouted and cried, as the fast-acting investors across the country sent their brokers scurrying out with sell orders.

The exchange ordered trading suspended in the stock until buy orders could be matched against sell orders. The stock was opened for trading the next day, down 19 points. (The sale of assets subsequently went through and the sellers in this case were not the fortunate ones.)

The Surface Elements of Price Pressures

Although this is an extreme case, it shows that stocks respond to the pressures of investors' purchases and sales. Because this emotional element is the obvious reason for price movements, a school of theorists has evolved a system of measuring public (or investor) interest in a particular stock that forecasts future price actions of that issue. This is the so-called "technician's" approach to stock-market price forecasting. The technicians use charts of price movements (daily), and the volume of stocks traded, over a period that may vary from 1 to 20 years back. By charting prices and volume in the past, a practical chartist can often forecast the timing of purchases and sales with great success. The primary purpose of the technical approach is to solve these problems of timing. The chartist is very often quite successful. The expert chartist will, however, usually combine a study of the performance data of the company to insure a margin of safety and then proceed to chart prices and volume to enable him to "buy low and sell high." The use of charts can be a fascinating and rewarding experience. Stocks do form very definite patterns of price action, but after a long period of fairly level price and volume ("an accumulation level," in the parlance of the chartist), a point in price slightly above the highest accumulation level is selected as the "break-out" level. By this is meant that, if the stock passes this price even fractionally, it will go up to new, higher levels. These levels are computed by the length of the accumulation level and prorated into a rising scale. The only problem in using charts exclusively is that, while one man may think it is an accumulation level, another may think it is a divesting level, where holders of shares are quietly selling out; in this instance, the break-out level may be on the "downside." It is the height of arrogance to dismiss charts as worthless, but it is the height of folly to rely only on the market price and volume of action of a stock to determine buying and selling decisions. Charts are a tool, not a machine: used cautiously, they can be helpful; used alone, they are dangerous.

Since stock prices move because of investors, the logical and basic question is: what moves investors?

THE FUNDAMENTALS THAT MOVE INVESTORS

This is the kernel of successful investing. The investor buys or sells stocks because of actual or anticipated *changes* in the operation of the company involved.

Understanding this seemingly simple fact must provide the key to long-term success in equity investments. By stripping away all the accumulated *dross* of rumors, hopes and myths, the investor who realizes what he is buying and why, has catapulted himself into the enviable world of reason and out of the morass of emotion.

What Is a Fundamentalist?

Most investors realize that their stock will perform only as well as the company which issued the stock. The school of investors that measures and weighs performance, markets, products, and management to determine investment decisions are called fundamentalists. They go beneath the ground-swells of market sentiment and base their moves into or out of a particular stock on the price of the stock in relation to the performance record of the corporation and the general market conditions.

The reasoning used is that, since all investors are seeking value, the fundamental investor will buy value and await the recognition of this value by other investors who come in later than he does. This may sound pompous, but it is not. There is not a wild attempt "to beat out the other guy." There is a conscious application of the rules of sound investing and a recognition that if your decision was indeed sound, other like-minded investors will recognize the same merits you have discovered.

Since stocks move in relation to earnings, it must be seen that earnings—sustained earnings—are the final arbiter of stock price action because investors have and will continue to respond to earnings. By evaluating a corporation from the standpoint of sales, cost of sales, profit margins, and earnings performance, you are in an excellent position to make a judgment as to merit and/or demerit of value.

Improved Fundamentals

In 1960, Lockheed Aircraft Corporation, completing a painful transition from airplane construction to aerospace technology and development, showed losses of $4.60 per share for the full year. Selling at $26.00 per share in early 1961, the company was showing remarkable signs of strength in earnings by July of the same year. Selling at $33.00 per share (some investors anticipated the return to profits), the stock was purchased at that price by many investors who were anticipating, with reason, full-year earnings of $3.00 per share. At the price of $33.00, or 11 times earnings for a company that was fully equipped to expand rapidly in the space age, this was good value, which was borne out by subsequent price action when the stock rose to $52.00. Investors will hold that stock until outside influence of serious magnitude (Government intervention) or earnings subside. They will be firm in their convictions, because 1962 earnings are running at a rate of $4.40, with a giant backlog of orders serving as a springboard for further earnings improvement.

The fundamental approach to stock purchase and sales is not just desirable but essential. There is no substitute for performance, and, to use an ancient cliché, the stock market is a market of stocks. Each is different; everyone has different problems and advantages. The factors influencing price performance are often so diverse as to be staggering, but by using the only yardstick available —performance data, and superimposing general knowledge thereon—risks are reduced and profit potential is enhanced.

The question of strong fundamentals as a basis for investing is very frequently derided by those who claim that, too often, you wind up sitting on safe but dull issues. Your money is invested in shares that don't move in price. Blind acceptance of the fundamental concept can result in this condition, except for one very important factor: *change*. This factor is what arouses interest, whether the change is for good or evil. Change in fundamentals will change prices either up or down.

Changing Fundamentals

United Fruit Company had been seriously stricken by adverse developments in the Caribbean, as well as by a decline in prices for its products— bananas. This former blue chip, largely held by "widows and orphans," had sold down to a price of $15.00 a share in 1961, following substantial losses a year earlier. This change in fortunes had resulted in a predictable result—a substantial drop in value of the stock.

In 1961, with new management and new programs, a change in earnings soon became apparent. Showing 50¢ earnings for the full year, the stock had returned to value of $23.00 by the fall of 1961. In early 1962, the stock went to $30.00, based on first-quarter earnings of 50¢.

These *changes* resulted in price movement, since it is axiomatic that stocks react to bad news and appreciate on good news.

Interplay of Fundamentals

Prospects for improved earnings for ABC Paramount were very good in early 1962. This major TV broadcasting system and theatre operator appeared ready to return higher earnings based on expanded advertising expenditures during a "good" business year. Selling at about $40.00 a share, prospects were encouraging for further improvement in earnings and hence in price. But in early 1962, the Congressional hearings on TV programming had dealt ABC a black eye. A shake-up in top management resulted in further loss of investor confidence. Reports that fall programming was not being snapped up by advertisers sent the stock down as low as $23.00. Predictable?—yes; though fundamentals are the cornerstone of successful buying, they also are the key to selling decisions. The fact of replacement of a top official may not constitute a change for the worse, and adverse publicity may be of only short-term impact, but the facts of decline in advertising revenue are not to be passed over easily.

Weakening Fundamentals

In the early Sixties, the steel industry was pulsating danger signals to investors. Bethlehem Steel was being anxiously watched to see if its dividend payment would be cut. Earnings had barely covered the required payment. There were healthy sighs of relief as the Beth Steel directors continued payment, but it was a signal of trouble. U.S. Steel was not improving earnings in 1961. Inquisitive investors who took a substantial look at the attrition in profit margins, the inroads of foreign steel, and the erosion of markets by aluminum replacements, became worried. All of these factors, plus increased labor costs, were of sufficiently alarming proportions to warrant the sale of steel stocks.

The attitude adopted by many investors in the face of these facts was: this is a basic industry, basic to the needs of the economy; it cannot go down without dragging everything down. There will be a good automotive year in 1962, and efficiency of plants has improved. No, I won't sell steel, especially Big Steel; it is too strong. (U.S. Steel had been over $100 a share on earnings of $3.07 per share in 1961, or at more than 33 times earnings.)

There is no stock of any company that is too big or too strong to stumble, and the stumble can be a violent one when the earnings multiplier is high.

Just as signals to buy should not be ignored, so are signals to sell not to be ignored at the peril of losses. U.S. Steel fell in price to a level of $52.00 in May 1962, or to 16 times its previous year's earnings. By June, the price was $41.00, and the end was not yet in sight.

INVESTORS BUY ON FUNDAMENTALS

Stock prices move because of investor interest, and investors buy or sell because of the "fundamentals" of an individual stock. It is with the fundamentals of the Undervalued with which we shall be concerned. The purchase of shares at low levels of price in relation to earnings offers, of and by itself, a measure of protection against substantial losses. If we incorporate the further requirements of a strong current asset position and a solid foundation of total assets, we are providing a further cushion against unexpected occurrences sending our stock into a quick bout with the bankruptcy courts. If, in addition, we are armed with a good management team that has been capable in the past of trimming costs or keeping them stable while increasing sales or profit margins, we are adding one more buffer against sudden dizzying drops in value.

The Undervalued method of stock purchase and sale is designed to provide *reasonable* protection against *substantial* loss by utilizing every possible protection to safeguard capital.

Most important after this protection is the diagnosis of the change that is occurring that will effect the rise in price necessary for profit.

Protection Plus Improvement

The Liquidometer Corporation is a case in point. Selling at a price of $9.00 per share in 1959, this manufacturer of gauges announced earnings had improved from a deficit of 80¢ to a profit of 70¢ in the first half of 1960. By utilizing the fundamentals available at that time to the public, a purchase with confidence could have been effected and the stock held to a price of $25.00 per share, at which time it split two-for-one and then proceeded to rise again from $12.00 to $18.00.

The reason for the rise: earnings improved and continued to improve for some time. By keeping abreast of the progress of the company, after the investigation that preceded purchase, the investor was able to wait to be told when to sell his shares. Did he buy at the bottom and sell at the top? Probably not, unless he was fantastically lucky, for the market does not wait for anyone. Liquidometer had most of the safety features that an astute investor looks for in assessing a corporation: it had a good history of survival since 1928; it had net current assets almost equal to its selling price; total assets almost double the selling price; in short, there was substance behind the company that would cushion the fall if the unexpected happened (and the unexpected can happen to any company at any time). The reason for looking at these factors of "protection" is that some of the examples used in this book involve companies that have been experiencing serious reverses in earnings. Because of the always present danger of the company sinking back in to the loss column, protection becomes important.

Decline Without Protection

For the sake of contrast, examine the record of another small company, which had appeared on the rolls of publicly held companies during the electronics boom of the Fifties. Dunn Engineering Company had been brought out at a price of $3.00 a share. Within a relatively short period, it had sky-rocketed to $75.00 and then split three-for-one. Selling for some months at the split price of $25.00, it began a downward drift, as the bloom wore off electronic issues in general, and as earnings failed to materialize. In October of 1961, the stock was selling at $9.00, and all that the company had were promising prospects: a limited line of products produced for the space age by a bright group of scientists. In late 1961, Dunn Engineering seemed on the brink of making important gains through acceptance of its products and the advantage of several sizeable contracts from major space suppliers. The company was extremely marginal financially, but many investors purchased shares on a speculative basis. There is not—nor should there be—anything wrong with speculating in stocks which *might* develop. But look at what happened to Dunn: it went from $9.00 to $14.00 in a mere matter of weeks, then eased back to $12½, rose again to $13.00, and then settled back below $12.00. Within several months, the stock was at $9.00, then below $9.00 to $8.00. From $8.00, it rebounded once to a little over $9.00, and then sank rapidly. At the price of $6.00, there were rumors of a management shake-up, subsequently confirmed. At a price of $4.00, there were rumors of the company applying for short-term financing from the banks. At $1½, there was free talk of bankruptcy. At $½, the bankruptcy seemed imminent. The protection of an investor against the threat of bankruptcy lies in book value, working capital, net current asset value minus long-term debt of the corporation.

Speculation is a vital part of every market; but speculations with the odds of success constructed in your favor are much easier to live with, and far more profitable over the long-term than those based on hopes. Dunn Engineering went from $9.00 to $14.00, and then to $½. There have been more severe losses in major stocks in one day, so perhaps the dollar losses are not so great; but to be wiped out of one's total investment is a far cry from sustaining a substantial loss. At least some option is left with the major stock. It can be sold at a loss and the funds reinvested elsewhere in a more promising issue; or, if strong reasons exist for believing the stock may go lower, a short sale may be instituted. (However, usually you're too late if you've held on that long.) The point to be made is that speculation based on constructive facts can be rewarding. We shall pursue instances in the Undervalueds where the *speculator* may buy a stock that is *promising improvement,* while an *investor* will wait for the promise to become *reality* before buying.

THE "OUTSIDE" FORCES WHICH AFFECT PRICES OF STOCKS

Bull Market

The discussion of stock price movement has been limited to the technical and the fundamental concepts of stock purchase. Since the Undervalueds are based almost entirely on the fundamentals of each individual stock, it may seem superfluous to go further afield into the area of the market in general. But since the impact of outside events is felt throughout every area of the market, the fundamental investor finds himself in the bewildering mists of overdiscounting. Widespread confidence on the part of investors has the effect— a pyramiding effect—of attracting new investors into already high-priced securities. The word "sell" becomes a foreign word as prices of favorite issues spiral up and marginal issues are carried up by the wave of enthusiasm. In these markets, which all of us have witnessed through the Fifties, the question of when to sell becomes largely a matter of prudence, where the value investor says, "I don't care if it does keep going up: 40 times or 50 times earnings cannot be sustained for long." The 100 times earnings stocks are the fast-paced racers that cause sleepless nights. Very often, investors who hold such issues will place orders to sell at 10 or 20 points below the existing market and continue to raise their limit if the price continues up.

Bear Market

What occurs in a "selling market" is something to behold. Paper profits which took years to build, recede witheringly in a period of weeks or months. Just as in bull markets enthusiasm begets more enthusiasm, so in "bear" (or selling) markets fear of losses begets more fear as selling continues. During such markets, good stocks will recede, as buyers avoid purchases and wait for the dust to settle. Vulnerable stocks that have risen to spectacular heights draw tremendous selling attention as fearful owners move in to sell before all their profits disappear. During such periods, the "multiplier," which had risen so sharply, starts to plummet as investors re-examine their worth. These selling markets are decapitators of high-price-to-earnings-ratio stock values.

The influences that are brought to bear in such markets are reflections of the fears, hopes, and confidence of investors in the future of the general economy, the political climate as it affects business, taxes, and inflation. The flow of gold reserves out of the country, which makes the dollar vulnerable to further weakness through foreign intervention, contributed largely to investor fears in the market sell-off of late 1961 and early 1962. Attacks on business profits by Government antitrust suits, blanketing by threat or actual suits many diverse companies and industries, added to these fears. A general sense of impending, socialist-oriented legislation gave rise to fears of further Government controls as the agricultural community was exposed to legislation that would result in their outright abdication of choice by complete Government control. Fear of the Government, fear of the devaluation of the dollar, fear of taking risks when so many outside influences attacked the freedom required for risk capital to use itself productively—in short, when serious investor fears outweigh investor expectations, the stock market reflects them in lower prices. Add to these fears a very real situation of stocks priced at absurdly high levels in relation to their performance, and the outside influences are viewed more as a trigger for the downturn than as a propellant.

Constantly Changing Influences

As is the case with "up" markets, the investor cannot exist in a vacuum. Current events affect his stocks currently. The investor must be aware of what is happening in the world of business, domestic legislation, and foreign affairs, for they can and do affect his investments. An example of this is the situation that occurred in the savings-and-loan stocks, which had enjoyed high favor with investors not too long ago. In January of 1962, the new Congress indicated that tax-reform legislation would receive top priority during that session. One item mentioned prominently was the fact that past exemptions of savings-and-loan reserve funds would be proposed for new taxes. This was a signal to sell savings-and-loan stocks, if not immediately, then whenever confirmation of this proposal was announced—keeping always in mind that if the market had already discounted this event, such a sale would be too late.

The fundamentals provide the foundation for your investing program. Continued attention to your stocks provides the safety line to protection of profit and minimizing of losses.

It was stated in the beginning of this chapter that two legs are required for substantial improvement in stock prices: improved earnings and improved multipliers. Since a change in the multiplier is largely a matter of conjecture, we must pin the bulk of any expectation on earnings.

THE "MULTIPLIER" FOR SUBSTANTIAL GAINS

By buying "earnings" at a low enough multiple to permit improvement, we have at the very least permitted ourselves the greatest opportunity for profits. If we purchase a stock at 12 times earnings of $2.00 a share (or $24.00), with an earning projection of $2.75 for the current year, we have built a sound bridge for gains. Since the stock is at 12 times earnings of $2.00, it is not unreasonable to expect that the multiplier will not go lower than 12; and it is reasonable to *hope* that when the full year's earnings of $2.75 are accomplished, the stock will still be selling at 12 times earnings, or $33.00 per share. *If,* in the meantime, the multiplier is increased by substantial investor interest to, say, 15 times earnings, our profit potential is then raised to 41. Safety and reason dictate that hopes for a multiplier improvement are not to be confused with facts of earnings.

Look now in the other direction and assume that, in May 1962, you purchased Minnesota Mining at $50.00, selling near its low for the year. Having earned slightly less than $1.50 per share in the previous year, it was purchased at 40 times earnings. Assume that earnings for 1962 improved by 20 per cent to show full-year earnings of slightly more than $1.80. If the multiplier remained constant, your shares would be selling at $73.00. Are prospects good for the multiplier to increase? Not very good, one would think, when substantial companies of equal merit can be purchased for much less. What about the risk of the multiplier being revised downward? The risks are very real that this could happen. The stock is certainly vulnerable to profit-taking by old investors and loss-cutting by more recent ones. If any adverse news breaks on Minnesota, the ability to predict where the new low would be is sketchy at best. If the news were really serious, it is not inconceivable that 10 to 20 times earnings could be the new multiplier.

SUMMARY OF SOURCES OF CORPORATE FACTS

Because information is of such great importance to the investor, let us illustrate some of the most fertile sources of general information.

For preliminary investigation work, the major financial services provide the single greatest concentration of statistical, product, and general business news, and usually are available at public libraries.

For current events and news relating to business, *The Wall Street Journal* provides an excellent daily digest of pertinent and interesting news and events. Major dailies of almost every city provide substantial financial news sections, often featuring syndicated financial columnists and widespread reporting of corporate as well as related business and international events.

There are also paid financial services, numbering in the hundreds, which attempt to provide definite information about every conceivable area of the stock market. These services vary greatly in quality, quantity, and cost.

The investor who is steeped in a basic understanding of stock price movements and the fundamentals of stock can avail himself very profitably of the wealth of information assembled and presented by securities brokerage firms. Using member firms of the New York Stock Exchange as a criteria, it is possible to receive detailed information on hundreds of stocks each year. Professional analysts are employed to provide customers of these firms as much information as possible at no cost.

The availability of economic forecasts from your bank is another source of general business and economic news, which will provide a good background for forming judgments.

The Undervalueds will describe the work involved in solving some investing problems. It will be seen that information is the key to success.

5

The Undervalued
Method of Security
Evaluation

A recitation of what steps are needed to investigate an Undervalued Stock, an explanation of why this method is utilized, and what is accomplished for the investor. This chapter explains the form and substance of the steps, and the stages of the investigation method.

The work of a securities analyst is to discover stocks that are headed up in price. All of the theory, financial background, education, and experience in the world are worthless if the result of his work does not pay off in profits. Infallibility is not demanded of the analyst, but the cold objectivity to recognize a mistake and recommend sale is required.

The analyst is a professional whose continuance in his job depends on his success. It is a demanding profession of "crystal-ball gazing" that discharges the myopic or cross-eyed from its ranks. Because of the necessity for keeping body and soul together, and the recognition that his daily bread depends upon performance, the analyst cannot depend on "hunches" or his "feel for the market." The "intuition" of the analyst is usually as bad as that of the rankest amateur; in fact, the less emotion involved in the business of security analysis, the better. Emotion only gets in the way of judgment, casting shadows which obscure facts. Emotion is anathema to the talented securities analyst.

How does the analyst find the stocks which he recommends, and what basis does he use for that recommendation? How does he know (or suspect) that the price is reasonable? What yardsticks does he use for continuing to remain in the stock? What tells him when to recommend sale?

Essentially, the analyst looks for a company which is earning money, selling at a price which is reasonable, giving strong indications of substantially improved earnings in the near future, enjoying a strong financial and asset condition, with an efficient and aggressive management team. That's all he looks for in the beginning. Having found this desirable company, he will follow its progress closely for any faltering or back-sliding from its promise. When and if such a stumble occurs, he will recommend sale.

The analyst cannot, in other words, throw darts at *The Wall Street Journal* in the morning and come up with his recommendations for the day. He does not sit and watch the ticker tape, seeing which stocks are "moving well" and submitting a recommendation to buy one of them. He does not read research recommendations of other analysts and submit them in lieu of his own choice (or, at least, we hope he doesn't!). The analyst brings to bear on the art of investing all of the "science" which is within reach. It is only because investing is as much art as it is science that the analyst is not infallible. Using every tool available, however, science will level out the vagaries of art over a long period of time and put the science investor away out in front in profits.

The science, or tools, which the analyst uses in his job are not hard to find; they are, in fact, available to a degree to all investors. The first of these is information—all of the facts available about the corporation. Second is the organization of those facts into meaningful order, and third is judgment made on the basis of the interpretation of the facts.

THE UNDERVALUED METHOD

This book details and demonstrates a workable, short system of *locating* potentially profitable stocks. It shows you where to find the information needed to evaluate the stock. It shows you what information to obtain, and what the significance of that information is. It shows you how to organize this information in stages that grow progressively more detailed, but permits—in fact, demands—discontinuance of the investigation at early cut-off points when danger signals appear. It shows you how to make reasonable projections of earnings on the basis of the information discovered. It shows you how to evaluate prices. It shows you how to evaluate the stock discovered—i.e., to exercise judgment on the basis of the facts. It shows you how to gauge when to sell or when to continue holding the stocks. It shows you how to put yourself in the position of making knowledgeable decisions about the stocks you own now as well as those you are contemplating buying.

The Undervalued method opens the door to profits because it presents a simplified method of "investigating before you invest." It can be applied to all stocks at all times to provide you with clarification of doubts, to give you a clearer view of risks, to enable you to determine if the chances for loss outweigh gains. It provides you with an excellent yardstick to measure the worth of recommendations submitted to you. Last—and perhaps first in our view—is the exposure of the method needed, to supply the vision necessary to see when the losing company at a depressed price is giving off dynamic signals of meaningful change—often overlooked, sometimes "Undervalued."

HOW THE UNDERVALUED METHOD WORKS

The solution of the problem of selection is the first task of the investor. The Undervalued Method starts with the premise that "change" (earnings, margin of profit, new products, etc.) in a corporation often signifies a change in value of the stock. To take advantage of this fact and to eliminate the impossible task of screening thousands of corporations, the public announcement by a corporation of a "change" is utilized as a *"signal"* to direct our attention to the suspect corporation. Assume, for example, that Endicott Johnson Corporation announces through the press that a reduction in wages has been achieved through negotiation with the local union. This announcement would serve to attract our attention to Endicott Johnson.

The First Look

Because we may be examining hundreds of stocks each year, it would be extremely wasteful to exert great effort and expend a great deal of time in investigating stocks which are not fit for investment because of high prices or poor earnings or cloudy futures and dismal pasts. It is the aim of this system to provide easy steps of elimination (because most of the stocks examined will be eliminated) requiring little time but providing sufficient evidence to warn us onward. The first look is a scanning stage incorporating five steps dealing with the externals of the company and a hint of whether it has enough financial strength to warrant further investigation. By looking at the price of the stock, its current earnings, and several other surface factors, you are capable of deciding whether to stop or go. If this is a high price in relation to earnings, you will stop immediately. These and other criteria for making decisions are detailed in the chapter covering the first and second look.

The Second Look

Assuming the first look at the stock held promise, you would then go to the second stage of the Undervalued Method. Just as an analyst starts to dig into the body of a corporation which has aroused interest, so, too, will you start to probe a little.

This step consists of six elements, all but one of which are concerned with the operation of the corporation as revealed by its financial statements. What we attempt to discover here is: "How does this company do its job?" By looking at sales figures, you can judge fairly well not only the direction which the company is taking but also whether or not it holds promise of improvement or decline.

There are only six steps in this second look and it too must be considered a preliminary or "elimination" stage in the investigation. You are taking a light jab at the corporation to see if you hit muscle or flab. Very often, the surface facts show up well but the underpinnings are rotted. Because your time is valuable, this brief step adds to your structure of facts and permits judgment to decide to stop in the face of weakness or continue to investigate in the face of strength.

The Third Look—This is a Work Step

Whereas the first look takes surface elements of the current appearance of the stock, and the second look probes for a look at the operation of the company and its operating performance for the previous two years, the third look is not light or jabbing. It consists of a hard examination of a four-year record of performance of the company and the stock.

The third look is designed to provide a complete four-year picture of the basic elements needed to make a reasoned judgment.

This step is only for those corporations which have successfully passed the test of the first and second looks. This is the stage where decision will be made to buy or stay away. This is the step which enables you to make reasonable projections of earnings and performance. This is the step which can tell you how the market will probably react to the stock price if these projections work out. This is the step which is thorough, time consuming, and well worth the effort when it is your hard earned money that will be laid on the line.

The third look is the step which should be used to evaluate all of your present securities. This is an investigation which can pay in helping you to make reasoned decisions.

As mentioned previously, the third look covers a four-year span of the corporation's performance. (Many analysts consider ten-year records the only safe way to investigate; however, four years should provide reasonable safety.) This step duplicates the elements covered in the first and second look and it covers a longer period of time. In addition, the third look, consisting of 13 steps, covers those elements of the basic structure of the company needed to provide a level of safety and sufficient information to permit the making of decisions.

The completion of the third look gives you a strong outline of the company's assets and liabilities, its operating performance in costs and margins of profit, the earnings record and what the "market" paid for the stock in times past, what the direction of sales and earnings is, and valid earnings projections. It provides you with a strong position to judge what is probably (there are always unknowns) going to happen to earnings, and more important, what is probably going to happen to the price of the stock.

Finally, the only gain to be made through investigation is the insight achieved into what will happen to the company's performance. If we have clear signs of the direction of change and reasonably clear estimates of the degree of change, it then becomes possible to make a fair estimate of how the stock market (other investors) will react to this change when it occurs.

Because quarterly reports and publications of significant changes of any nature during the year enable you to maintain surveillance of your newly purchased stock, continuing evaluation is simple and profitable.

This is the professional's method of investing. Because of limitations of time and money, all of us cannot afford the luxury of hiring a personal professional analyst. Because of the importance of making sound investments, none of us can afford not to investigate.

The Undervalued Method is an abbreviated method designed to provide you with the knowledge needed to invest with confidence.

6

The Signal

A summary of the general area of corporate announcements. The possible significance of a particular signal is explained under five broad segments of the corporate whole.

THE ELEMENTS OF CHANGE

Companies, like people, do not change overnight. All the worthwhile changes are generally preceded by alterations within the company, its products, or markets, which are designed to provide higher earnings.

There are very seldom legitimate "windfalls" of high profits in business. It is the calculated decision of management which decides growth or contraction.

Decisions taken in 1954 by several of the air frame manufacturers started bearing fruit in 1961. Decisions made in the late Forties by the management of Montgomery Ward started the contraction of earnings for the company in the Fifties.

The day-to-day changes, which often go unnoticed as part of our existence and changing times, are often very significant in leading the investor into investment situations. The widely publicized baby boom in the early post-World War II years, carrying through the Korean War, resulted in rocketing sales and consequent price gains in school equipment stocks, toy stocks, and record company stocks. The curve of juvenile equipment stocks paralleled juvenile growth. Future and continuing impact of this bulge in the population will be felt as these children grow, marry, and buy homes, autos, insurance, and so on.

CORPORATION "LOOK" SIGNALS

The economy gives off signals to investors. The signals with which we shall concern ourselves are much more prosaic than an international crisis. They are the signals of individual corporations.

The public corporation assumes certain obligations by being "public," not the least of which involves full disclosure of its operations. These disclosures are not so rigid as to impede the competitiveness of a company, but they are complete enough to give an investor a clear picture of what he is buying. It is the public character of the company that occasions notification by the board of directors, to the press and stockholders, of information about actions planned or taken, and results achieved or expected. These announcements by management are the "signals to look" at the stock.

The Public Announcement of "Signals"

This notification is of such value that the types and character of this public information will be investigated in some detail.

The importance of a signal is *not* the context of the announcement. This point bears some emphasis. The notification of a proposed change in capitalization of the Bon Ami Corporation detailing the proposal to eliminate all class B shares in a newly formed single class of common stock would have little or no meaning to the casual reader.

Yet capitalization changes are made for a reason. Why do directors wish to eliminate one class of stock? Why tinker with capitalization at all? When all is said and done, the seeker of Undervalued Stocks does not really care what the meaning of this proposal is *at this time*. He has seen a public announcement of a *change* (proposed) in capitalization. The result of this recognition of a signal should be to take a look at Bon Ami Corporation. The first look is all that is needed. There is no computation necessary, no detailed work. Just look at the surface elements of the stock.

The first goal of the signal is to attract your attention to the stock. The secondary value of the announcement is the context or meaning of the announcement. In the case of Bon Ami, the proposal, when it was voted upon by shareholders, resulted in elimination of the class B stock. This stock was actually a preferred issue with cumulative dividend obligations attached which had acted as a severe drag on the corporation's earnings, and indeed created swollen deficits during the many lean years of the company's recent history.

The investor who was looking for value, however, would not have given any weight to the significance of this proposal until: (1) the proposal was an accomplished fact; and (2) the examination or third look was completed, at which time the benefits would be added to the other facts discovered, to influence judgment.

The signal as an indicator is of primary value in that it serves to focus our attention on the stock. The *meaning* of the signal can often be of great value when added to the final step of examination.

THE VARIETY OF SIGNALS

Signal flags are as diverse and varied as the problems and products of industry. To highlight some possible signals and their *possible* meaning we shall examine some of the more common public announcements.

In order to facilitate the examination, to put it in perspective, a basic structure of all corporations is used to indicate the particular area of the corporate whole which is affected by the signal.

Every corporation has five parts. Whether it be a billion dollar giant or a tiny 10-man shop, the same elements are present, and the problems are often the same.

These corporation parts consist of:

(1) Physical Plant Signals—plants, materials, equipment, and the men to fabricate the products of service.

(2) Product Signals—distribution of all products which includes sales force, and transportation, etc.

(3) Management Signals—administration (management).

(4) Capitalization Signals.

(5) Miscellaneous Signals—covering outside forces which can, or might, affect the whole structure, including the all-important area of research and development.

Physical Plant Signals

The much talked of squeeze on profits which has been such a bone of contention between labor, management, and, in recent years, Government, is the direct result of operational costs increasing while prices either remain steady, or increase in a smaller ratio. The corporation which can pare costs even while sales remain static is doing just as effective a job as the much heralded company which announces proudly that "sales will be up 25 per cent this year," ignoring the little matter of costs. The wide-eyed investor discovers the fact that costs went up more than 25 per cent and actual earnings declined. The corporate structure frequently provides significant signals, mainly those relating to costs—i.e., plants, equipment, and personnel.

The announcement that Lilly Tulip Corporation has purchased land in Holindel, N.J., for the purpose of constructing a new plant to produce plastic products, is a signal. Announcement of extensive cost-cutting by the management of Chrysler Corporation in 1961 is a signal. The difference between these two new announcements lies in the fact that one was a long way off (the plant), whereas the other was already accomplished. Both, however, were signals of a change.

(The savings involved in moving to new facilities can be significant in improved earnings.)

Of the elements of production, there is no doubt that in most instances wage costs are generally the greatest contributors to costs, and most often the least flexible. Because wage contracts are often based on the geographic area, as well as the peculiarities of the plant involved, it becomes possible to move to a newer plant in a different area and achieve the savings denied in the old area. The unfortunate circumstances surrounding abandonment of otherwise adequate facilities because of rigid union demands has become so frequent in recent years as to cry out for a more rational approach to wage negotiations.

The area of labor relations is a highly specialized one. The details of a wage contract, with built-in increments of increase each year, as well as the often nebulous fringe benefits, with their possible effects on earnings, are not easily subjected to analysis. The long-term strike at Westinghouse, several years ago, left that corporation in a greatly weakened competitive condition. The steel strike in 1960, with its heavy impact on annual earnings, is but one of the few memorable labor difficulties which adversely affected earnings and stock prices.

The increased wage cost settlement must be viewed against the margins of profit of the corporation in prior years, adjusted for the new percentage of increase in wages. If there is no increase in prices and/or no cut-backs in the labor force, then earnings will very probably be narrowed.

The new plant, equipment, or wage settlement signals are seemingly the dullest of the possible investigation areas outlined here, but as is so often the case, they are only dull because they are so basic. The glamourous new product is much more exciting than a new plant, but consider the effect of two construction projects which had differing results. Phelps Dodge Corporation decided in the Thirties to integrate its copper mining business and proceeded to build its own smelting plants. This decision, made many years ago, left Phelps during the Fifties with a relatively small investment largely written off. Competitors such as Anaconda Copper faced huge capital outlays to effect the same result during the Fifties. Yet another decision by Phelps, also during the Fifties, to continue this process of integration, was to construct copper fabricating plants. Some $50,000,000 invested in tube and wire plants have not proved profitable during the early Sixties, largely because of overcapacity in the industry and consequent competitive price cutting.

The mechanics of business translated into the prices of stocks is an obvious relationship, but the fundamental approach to securities investment is predicated on this relationship. The public announcement vehicle for riding toward undervalued stocks is based on this premise: that statements announcing *changes* in the business may herald *changes* in earnings, and since *change* is what investors respond to, it follows that the signal is the most appropriate avenue for locating stocks.

Product Signals

The next area of the corporate structure is that of products. The signals about products are vast in scope. They may comprise new products, or variations of old ones, new markets or even new packaging. Revised or unique advertising campaigns may be a sufficient signal to capture attention—the field of products, the sales and merchandising of those products, is another severe test for management.

In 1961, Technicolor Corporation was being talked about because of a new venture into an 8 mm. movie camera. The stock responded to this yet-to-be-marketed new product, and rose to a price of 38 (from 16). In early 1962, the product had been marketed and the stock was down to 13.

On the other hand, E. F. MacDonald Corporation, which is in a service business of providing premiums to industry for incentive contests, received in 1961 a contract to supply "trading stamps" to the Great Atlantic and Pacific food stores. The future increase in earnings for MacDonald was quickly discounted as the stock rose from 19 to over 100 in a six-month period.

There is not much doubt that the "new" product or development can and does have the most valuable effect on stock prices in the shortest time. The great danger in accepting the context of this signal without investigation is that "many developments fail to develop." This is the era where rumor has the greatest field day. The surging emotions of investors are reflected in stock prices as hopes soar on rumors and crash resoundingly on ultimate failures or disclaimers of the hoped-for new developments.

In the products and merchandising category are the often overlooked but all-important sales and distribution methods used by the corporation. Since the employment of salesmen (as against the utilization of agents or distributors) can have sizeable effect on costs of sales, the announced changes from direct selling to agency or vice versa may serve as a signal worth checking. The expansion of a company into new markets with its products is illustrated by the company which effected an agreement with a food chain to utilize food stores as sales offices for its products (Aldens Corporation). Licensing agreements, mergers, or acquisitions result, or may result, in substantial changes in outlook and performance for a corporation. It sometimes happens that a company being acquired is a more immediately profitable stock purchase than the acquiring company stock. The merger trail is one that has been well worn in recent years: Philco absorbed by Ford, Sylvania by General Telephone, Ling Tempo purchasing control of Chance Vought. American Viscose, with limited markets for increasing sales of existing products, seeks new products. W. R. Grace Company, with its sensationally successful chemicals, was seeking survival from shrinking profits in shipping. However, mergers pose problems which in many instances do not lend themselves to easy solutions. Ryder System, a truck and auto leasing company, expanded very rapidly and saw earnings shrink as the digestion period resulted in some indigestion.

Sometimes, management skilled in one field jumps into an unknown product area and falls flat on its face as inexperience shows an ugly result in earnings. These unknowns, in otherwise sound situations, are the risk elements of investing in expanding companies—expanding outside their fields. This risk factor merely serves to reinforce the protection elements of sound financial and operating condition in the acquiring corporation before investing.

Management Signals

The advent of the age of automation has prompted many theorists to envision a world where machines take over many of the functions of man. One area not susceptible to automation is judgment. Management is judgment. Whether it be managing a family, a social group, a small business, or a giant corporation, the very human quality of judgment is something no machine can supply. The successful corporation of today is no more than the result of the continued and continuing success of management.

Management signals can be the most significant but least easy to interpret of all corporate changes.

The management change in Chrysler Corporation in 1961 was greeted by most investors with a sigh of relief. Executive change as well as some changes in the board of directors were welcomed after the previous management had succeeded in improving losses as well as decreasing market penetration of the corporate products. Rocked by a scandal as well as losses, this well-publicized management change, in the view of the financial community, was a hopeful one.

The immeasurable benefits of a strong new leader at the helm of a company that is in the doldrums can be subtle and startling. The major force that turns a company from losses to earnings is management—sometimes new management, sometimes old management with a new view imparted by the yawning abyss of losses.

The sometimes overused term "management" is one which is measured in the ever-unfolding facts of performance. The harsh statistics of sales, costs, and earnings are the tools of investors to weigh decisions: buy—sell—hold.

Capitalization Signals

If management is the key to success, capital is the door and the lock. The signals about capital are more plentiful than any others—the financial press abounds with them. The capitalization of a corporation is the sum total of par or stated value of shares outstanding. The capital stock is that which is authorized for sale to raise capital for the corporation. Although a company may have authorized (by its charter and by-laws) five million shares, the amount of stock outstanding may be only two million. The outstanding shares are those which have been sold. With several classes of stocks, the capital "structure" builds up to another level. In many instances when a company first "goes public," the old owners of the company reserve certain prerogatives for themselves—cumulative dividends, or the only voting shares, for example. Mounted on top of the common stock may be a preferred stock issue. Preferred stock is generally issued, not as a debt, but as an equity investment with a variety of attached conditions: convertibility into common, a fixed interest payment which may or may not be cumulative, a call feature whereby the corporation reserves the right to recall the stock at a stipulated redemption price. There may be several classes of preferred at different par values. The next step in the structure is the debt of the corporation, generally consisting of bonds. These bond obligations represent money borrowed on the basis of collateral (mortgage or equipment bonds), and debentures which are backed by the promise to pay by the borrowers. These debentures are comparable to a promissory note and may carry some extra incentive benefits such as convertibility.

The importance of capital change signals is evident when consideration is given to the fact that many, if not most, major changes for any corporation require capital in sizeable amounts. Requests by the board of directors to the shareholders for permission to increase the number of shares authorized may be a first step in plans to expand the corporation through acquisitions with payment made in stock, or it may be a prelude to voting stock dividends to shareholders. Though the ultimate use of the new financing or capital structure change may be obscure, keep in mind that in the selection process the importance of the signal is the fact that our attention is drawn to the company.

MISCELLANEOUS SIGNALS

Outside forces affect a company almost as often and sometimes more violently than the internal waves of change. Most common in these days of neo-socialism are Government actions. It is almost axiomatic that, when the Government involves itself with an industry or a particular company, the chances for stock-price improvement are reduced by a healthy percentage. The reasons for this are self-evident in light of the facts that investors constantly "anticipate" (discount) events affecting corporations. When a suit is brought against a company by the Government, investors anticipate that the suit will: (1) take a long time to settle; (2) act as a drain on capital through high costs of specialized attorneys; (3) divert management from going through with planned capital outlays for new plants, equipment, etc.;

(4) possibly result in sizeable fines or marketing restrictions on the companies if the Government wins.

The effect on drug company stocks during a Congressional investigation of drug profits was to depress the price of these shares. Price-fixing charges culminating in convictions against several major electrical equipment manufacturers left those stocks under continuing pressure, as customers filed damage suits against the concerns involved. Charges of profiteering against defense contracting companies brought down the wrath of investors on defense stocks. Antitrust suits have become so frequent that investors are getting somewhat blasé about them. Moves by the Government to divest General Motors of its automobile financing subsidiary (G.M.A.C.) have not as yet adversely affected General Motor's stock.

The 14-year struggle to have DuPont distribute its sizeable General Motors shares had slight long-term effect on the stock of either company. As a general rule, when there is a major involvement with the Government, it is a strong signal to stay away. For the same reasons as with proxy fights, it must be recognized that, with all of the problems involved in selecting securities in good health, it is near financial suicide to add more risk to an already risky capital venture.

Outside the area of Government are the signals of court suits for or against the company. It sometimes happens that when large damage suits are pending against a corporation, the price of the stock will stay quite static. Settlement of these suits may find an Undervalued Stock. Long-standing orders of restraint, when raised, are possibly valuable signals. The entire area of natural disasters, a hurricane's effects on insurance company stocks, for example, can produce sudden drops in value of these shares.

One of the very important elements which has characterized America's industrial growth has been "R & D"—Research and Development. "Yankee ingenuity" in the early years of the Republic was a less-glamorized version of our modern research and development work but not any different in structure and purpose.

The "signals" relating to R & D are fantastic in number, scope, and difficulty of analysis, but they often represent equally fantastic profit opportunities.

The U.S. industrial colossus, much maligned by the socialist-oriented groups, is a masterpiece of production, efficiency, and, more than that, a colossal tribute to the vision and courage of industrial managers who risked tremendous amounts of time, money, and effort on the development of the "new." Because the results of success are profits, the dreamers of the world point an accusing finger, but the development of entire new industries, life-saving drugs, thousands of new jobs, and the opening of vast new areas for further gains have

come not from the State, which is a consumer of wealth, but from industry, √
which is a producer of wealth—wealth in its true sense, not of dollars but of
things of value.

Research and development can change the complexion and outlook of a
single company or an entire industry almost overnight. Nylon by DuPont is still
opening the way to further changes in many industries. New Silicone developments may revive the long dormant copper industry by providing thousands of
new uses for the red metal. Thermal units may be the future source of power
production. The Buck Rogers dreams of yesterday are close to reality today.
Television has accounted for a tremendous change in industry and at home
with more and better improvements to come. Polaroid and Xerox are two gleam-
ing examples of research and development in the profit-and-loss column.
"Metrecal for the weight conscious" is an example of the not-so-glamorous product which can send the price of its developer (Mead Johnson & Co.) into the
upper price ranges of the stock market.

Research and development signals can be very strong medicine for the
fortunes of a corporation and for your own fortunes. They can also be extremely
disappointing, because so few of the thousands of new products ever succeed.
Do not place as much hope on the new development as you do on the fundamentals of the corporation. Publicity releases are not legal tender backed by
the full resources of the U.S. Government, so treat them seriously but invest
in the corporation and not in its press releases. Invest in the future with confidence in the continuance of free enterprise and the genius of man, but water
your enthusiasm with facts.

FINDINGS

The rather brief exposition of signals covered in this chapter is merely
a highlight of the areas in which corporations "made news." The use of signals
as beacons to search out worthwhile investment stocks is an invigorating experience which will open new areas. The surprise of finding solidly based investment situations will frequently be overshadowed by the pleasure of profits
earned by diligence and acumen.

7

A Close Look
at the First Stages
of the Investigation

Each step in the first look is covered in detail. Explanation of the meaning of the step and its significance to the investor is covered.

The first look at a stock which has emitted a signal is a fast look. It is used to tell the investor whether or not a stock is low enough in price in *relation* to its earnings to afford the prospect for gain. Primarily used to save time and effort, this step affords sufficient information to enable a judgment to be made whether or not to continue investigating.

The conclusions reached as a result of the first look are preliminary. Going back to the reasons why stock prices move, it was stated that, though investors move prices by buying or selling, underlying that fact is the motivation for them to buy or sell.

Investors respond to *changes,* real or anticipated, which affect earnings. Since earnings are the ultimate criteria, our first look merely gives us the surface position of a company.

THE FIRST LOOK

Step *1—Price*

The price of the stock at the time of the signal is the first item. The daily newspaper is the source of the day's closing price of the new-found suspect. The price of a stock standing alone means very little to us because there is nothing to measure this price against to determine value. Knowing nothing of the company's products, prospects, or performance, price merely stands as a representation of what some willing buyer decided that day to have been good value. Price, however, is the first measure we have to relate to other facts which we will later uncover.

Step *2—Earnings*

The goal and driving force behind every job in every industry in the country is earnings. The most humble clerk and the most high-powered executive each devote their working day to the achievement of this end. Since the time Adam and Eve were cast out of the Garden of Eden, mankind has been sentenced to earning bread by the sweat of his brow. In the modern world of the Welfare State, what was once a noble end—individual profit, earned by honest industry—has become warped and stigmatized as a shameful goal, based on the corrupt use of economic tools. (Because earnings are the lifeblood of a free, competitive economy, it will be a severe blow to the continuance of the free society if individuals and corporations are so hampered by restrictions that continuance in business becomes unprofitable.)

Earnings are the measure of success and the strength for continuance in a free economy. The free economy casts aside the ill-managed, the corrupt, the unprofitable corporation, recognizing that mistakes must be corrected, and correcting them, in many instances, through the attrition of failure. If a company fails to make money consistently, it must one day close its doors and go out of business. Hard? Yes. Just? Yes. Contrast the operation of a free economy, where mistakes are corrected in this manner, with a controlled economy where inefficient businesses are subsidized by tax dollars without regard to efficiency.

Most companies report earnings quarterly. The current period earnings report is made with the comparison report of how the company fared during the same period of the previous year. By taking the current period (the most recent quarterly report issued), together with the earnings for the two most recent full years, we have a valuable aid in giving us the trend in earnings. In the Undervalued Stock, it is the direction of earnings as well as the amount of earnings which trigger interest. The company which has been losing substantial amounts and which shows *significant declines* in the *amount of losses* is another valid candidate for the title of Undervalued. The same thing may be said for the company which has been static in performance and is giving signs that substantial improvements are in sight.

The single greatest factor in all the steps of the Undervalued is earnings. Not just this year's, or this quarter's earnings, but the company's history of earnings. For a number of years, Schenley Corporation traded within the range of $18.00 to $27.00 per share (from 1953 to 1957). The company made substantial amounts of money and paid out dividends of $1.00 per share. The stock did not appreciate considerably because earnings were dull. There were no significant changes in view, so investors watched and waited.

Schenley's earnings ran from a low of 87¢ to a high of $2.70 during the five years 1953 through 1957. Contrast that with Xerox Corporation, the manufacturer of photo copy machines: Allowing for stock splits in 1957 and 1958, the company earned 46¢, 49¢, 60¢, 67¢ and $1.40 in each year 1957 through 1961. The price of the stock ranged from 68¼ to 171⅝ in 1961 on the earnings of $1.40. Insane prices? There isn't too much doubt that 120 times earnings is dangerous in the extreme, but looking under the bare prices, the primary reason which created the extreme demand for this stock was the "foreseeable" earnings of $4.00 to $4.50 per share in 1962. Even when these earnings are achieved (assuming there are no undesireable experiences during this period), the stock was selling at 40 times earnings ($160 per share with earnings of $4.00). This does look a bit rich and could hardly be called Undervalued. The fact that stocks get overvalued is the element which permits profits, so there is no attempt to influence the constant interplay which takes place in a free market. There is no attempt here to fix arbitrary rules for earnings or earnings trends. Each individual stock is a story in and of itself. The static earnings for one company may be the pause preceding the great leap forward. For another it may be the tired gasp of an exhausted company preceding a downhill slide. These are the factors which preclude making judgments on the basis of insufficient facts. Earnings are important, but the underlying facts which tell a bigger story are the ultimate basis for judgment.*

Step 3—The Price Earnings Ratio

Just as a businessman contemplating purchase of a company will examine the plants, product, and facilities of his prospective purchase, when it comes to a discussion of terms, the yardstick of earnings will loom large in the negotiations. If, for example, the company "on the block" has earned an average of $25,000 for five years on net assets of $200,000, the purchaser will figure that, if he paid $200,000 for the company (or asset value), it would take him eight years to recover his investment (neglecting interest payments and other costs for this illustration). This is assuming earnings are unchanged during that period. However, the vicissitudes of business, incorporating the constant threat of the unexpected, would doubtless move our buyer into bargaining for a lower price. He would perhaps offer five times the annual earnings, or $125,000, and attempt to reduce his risk, but regardless of the outcome of our hypothetical case, it must be clear that the investor who purchases stocks is in the same position as the businessman. There is perhaps nothing more nebulous than the price earnings ratio: Standard Oil of New Jersey, a royal blue chip, sold at 12 to 15 times earnings (earnings of $3.50, price range 40¾ to 52) during 1961, while American Photocopy sold at 35 to 63 times earnings (earnings of 72¢ for the year, price range 25½ to 46) during the same year. Reason rebels against such a disparity in valuation of two companies, which enjoy such a wide gulf in earnings, asset values, and stability, but second thoughts indicate what is taking place.

The stable earnings corporation can be illustrated by looking at "Jersey

---

* See Appendix: "Nonrecurring Income and Losses."

Standard." It is a well-known, reliable company whose performance and expected performance are fairly well known. Relative stability has been achieved and investors know that the dividend (currently $2.50, with some dividend paid each year since 1882) is safe and that very probably earnings will improve (as they did in 1960 and 1961) as the financial strength and top-flight management bring about solutions to the growth problem of the oil industry. Thus, because there are so many known factors surrounding the company, because earnings had declined for several years (1958 and 1959) from the 1957 level of $3.96 per share, because there was little "glamour" attached to the industry or the company, the market disdainfully left Jersey (and most of the other oils) at low earnings multiple. Thus an investor who contemplated purchase of Jersey when it was at 15 times earnings was putting up an obstacle to appreciation in price. If the historic price earnings is 12 to 15 times—this can change and, in the case of selected oil stocks, it probably will in view of the long-term outlook for increased demand for oil and oil products in Europe and the Far East—then the investor who purchases the stock at 12 times earnings is picking up a double-edged sword. With earnings of $3.50, this would be a $42.00 purchase price. If earnings go up to $4.00 and the multiplier remains constant, then the price should reach $48.00, but the investor has reasonable grounds for *hoping* that the multiplier will travel to 15 times earnings of $4.00, or a price of $60.00. Admittedly, these are not hard and fast rules, but the point to be remembered is that a change in earnings and a constant multiplier should result in *some* gains; but a change in multiplier (even a slight one), coupled with a change in earnings, can result in substantial gains even in the so-called non-glamour issues.

The high price earnings stock can be seen by examining American Photocopy. In the case of this stock, a purchase made at 25½ or 35 times earnings is fraught with risk. There is the ever-present risk that the market will re-evaluate the multiplier downward. A decrease in earnings is not too vicious a loss if the multiplier remains constant, but a downward revision of the multiplier can be a sleigh ride to disaster. Because investors are not stupid, it would be a mistake to condemn high price earnings ratios out of hand. In almost every instance, the glamour stock is glamorized because of its *potential* earnings. Adjusting earnings for stock splits (split three-for-one in 1959 and again in 1961. American Photocopy Company earned 26¢ in 1957, 30¢ in 1958, for a growth rate of slightly better than 15 per cent. In 1959, earnings were 47¢, or an apparent growth rate of 56 per cent; but a note advises that this figure includes some extraordinary income: i.e., nonrecurring capital gains, so that the huge gain is somewhat negated. In 1960, earnings were 57¢ for a gain of almost 22 per cent; and in 1961 the company showed 72¢ for another increase of 12 per cent. If the company could continue to grow at a 20 per cent rate compounded then in three years, or 1964, earnings would be approximately $1.30 per share. If you bought at 25½, or the lowest price in 1961, you paid 20 times the earnings projected three years in the future. The market has always, and doubtless will continue to put a premium on growth. New industries and new products carry risks, and for those risks premium prices are often paid because the return can be high.

The stock selling at 18 times earnings, which has the potential of increasing its earnings, and the future potential of going to 25 times earnings, may be a good value. The stock at eight times earnings with prospects of slight improvement in earnings, and the promise of staying at eight times earnings, may be a poor value. But it must be kept in mind that the low price to earnings stock which seems "dull" will not be ignored by the market if substantial changes take place in its earnings outlook and performance.

Continuance of earnings performance must be added to the elements of the price earnings multiplier. Surprise is sometimes expressed when a company making substantial earnings starts to decline in price. This will occur if suspicions are aroused that changes are occurring which will preclude continuance of those earnings.

The price earnings multiplier is a key step in the first look at the Undervalueds because it is so revealing about whether the stock under investigation has a sufficiently low multiplier of earnings to afford room for an improvement in that multiplier. We shall not set arbitrary limits on the ideal multiplier for a possible Undervalued, because of the tremendous variance allowed and allowable from one industry to another, and indeed from one company to another. It will be much more intelligible to use as a point of reference the examples subsequently illustrated. Another reason for not fixing hard-and-fast rules on the multiplier is the fact that on occasion the entire market wiggles, writhes, and painfully readjusts the old P.E. ratios to new, lower levels. There are other occasions when particular industries are singled out for multiplier revamping, either up or down. It is these changes which occasion the gnashing of teeth, or jumps for joy. The philosophy underlying the Undervalueds is to buy the stock for and on its merits, not because of the industry price earnings ratio.

Step 4—Number of Shares Outstanding

Why look at this at all? What possible difference could it make to us whether there are one million or five million shares outstanding?

In one sense, it doesn't really matter, but for purposes of the Undervalueds, it matters for two reasons. First, the number of shares available for trading has a great influence on the volatility of price fluctuations. If there are few shares outstanding, then changes in demand or in selling will result in sharp changes in price. If, on the other hand, huge blocks of stock are outstanding, the available supply will normally be plentiful and price movements relatively stable. Also present is the danger that exists in the Undervalueds of seeking small companies with too few shares outstanding to permit the making of a fair market in the stock.

Another and perhaps more important reason is the fact that we are interested in computing some values on a per share basis. This is the case with earnings and the net current asset values which form a part of the first step. The number of shares outstanding is the pivot off which we relate the asset values and other operating data of the corporation.

The place of the common stock in the capital structure is the base of that edifice. The importance of the per share figure is even more obvious when it is seen that stock prices are based largely on per share earnings, thus a Riddle Airlines with over 13,000,000 shares outstanding must earn sizeable dollar amounts to show any substantial per share earnings, while Liquidometer Corporation with slightly more than half a million shares can show considerably higher per share earnings on substantially fewer dollars in earnings. This is not to be construed as a reason for seeking only companies with few shares outstanding, but to demonstrate the practical effects of "Number of Shares Outstanding" on prices and on stock evaluation.*

Step 5—*Net Current Asset Value per Share Less Long Term Debt*

This rather pompous-sounding phrase contains the first qualitative test for the stock under examination. The purpose of examining this item is to determine if the company has the wherewithal to continue in business. Just as the bank wants to get quite nosey about our financial position when we attempt to borrow some of their depositors' monies, so it is with the investor who is contemplating sinking his own hard-earned dollars into a company's stock. The net current assets per share give us the approximate amount of dollars which the company could come up with in a hurry. Since a company can only pay its bills in cash, we do not wish to take the risk of investing in a firm which is stretched so tight financially that if all its creditors (current) were to demand payment at the same time, the company would be out of funds and forced to resort to: (1) expensive short-term financings; (2) mortgaging fixed assets; or (3) if unable to accomplish either, be faced with reorganization or bankruptcy (voluntary or otherwise). The net current asset value per share tells us how capable an industrial company would be in weathering adversity for the long or short term.

---

* See Appendix: "Floating Supply of Stock."

Dynaelectron Corporation, in 1961, showed current assets of $9,760,000, with current liabilities of $9,360,000, leaving net current asset total of $400,000. This relationship of what is owned (current) to what is owed (current) is so close as to be dangerous to the company and hence to investors. With 2,446,000 shares outstanding, the company has a net current asset value per share of a meager 16¢ against a stock value of 2½ to 3 per share during 1961. The investor should not purchase shares in companies which do not have sufficient financial strength to survive even short periods of adversity.

The net current asset value of a company consists of two elements. Current assets are those assets which, from accounting and business experience, can be converted into cash or credit with relative ease and in a short time; hence "current." Assets such as cash and marketable securities are obvious candidates, but beyond these are accounts receivable, which can be sold to factoring or other credit firms at substantial discounts from the amount shown as due, and inventories * which, *theoretically*, can be disposed of quickly.

There may in some instances be other items, such as prepaid expenses, carried as current assets, with the realization that such expenses may be partially recovered if the goods or service contracted for are not utilized.

The total of these items constitute current assets. *Liabilities* is the other element in our resultant "net." Most liabilities are "current" liabilities unless specified "long term." Long-term liabilities are those which are repayable over a fixed period of time, usually two years or longer, with fixed increments of repayment. These liabilities are usually bonds or long-term bank loans. All other liabilities are current. Current liabilities consist of wages and salaries due employees, accounts payable to suppliers of the companies raw materials, all expenses such as advertising, sales promotion, taxes, maintenance and repairs, supplies, fuel, power—anything and everything which must be paid to enable the company to continue in business.

By taking the sum total of current assets less current liabilities, we arrive at a net current asset value. For the purposes of the Undervalueds, we also deduct long-term debt from this net figure, resulting in a clear picture of how well-off the candidate corporation really is.

This dollar total may be of an impressive size (as was Dynaelectron's $400,-000), but dollar size is only relative to the demands made on the company. To add perspective to this figure, we relate it to the number of shares outstanding (just the common stock for our purposes). If we find a stock selling at $6.00 with current assets in pennies, we would steer shy. Primary concern is given to safety, and safety requires that if something goes wrong in the company, it

---

* See Appendix: "Liquidity of Assets."

must have sufficient reserve strength to surmount the crisis. Without money, it cannot do this. When all of the terminology of accounting is boiled down, the answer still must be "enough money to pay the bills."

Though net current asset value per share is usually revealing enough to inform the investigator whether to desist or continue with the Undervalued examination, there is one further item which can and should be used—the net current ratio, which is merely a look at the same two elements of current assets and liabilities as they relate to each other. Where Dynaelectron in 1961 had a ratio of approximately one-to-one (9.73 to 9.46 million), Standard Screw Company showed a much healthier 3.7-to-1 ratio (current assets $20.1 million versus current liabilities of $5.7 million). As a rule of thumb, a net current ratio of less than one-to-one would be a sign of danger.

SUMMARY

The first look is quite painless but also quite instructive. The steps, in order, are:

1. Price.
2. Earnings (two full years plus the current period).
3. Price earnings ratio.
4. Number of shares outstanding.
5. Net current asset value per share less long-term debt.

Given this information, we are put on speaking terms with a stock. The *first three steps* together give us a picture of the relative value of the stock and indicate whether it is sufficiently "low" in price to warrant continuance.

The *second step* has supplied a clue as to the current trend in earnings. If the trend is down or level and the price is fairly "rich" in relation to these earnings, we would discard the stock. If, on the other hand, the figures are strong in these areas, we would determine *Step 4—the number of shares* outstanding to use primarily as a tool for computing *net current asset value per share less long-term debt (Step 5)*. If *Step 5* shows some muscle, or possibly even some fat, there is every reason to move on to the second look.

The first look is preliminary, a mere scratching at the door of the Undervalueds, with the twofold aim of confirming action or unmasking the overpriced stock.

AN EXAMPLE OF THE FIRST LOOK AT WORK

In the case of the sample used, the Standard Screw Company, the price was found to be 22½ bid, 23½ asked. Using the *first look*, our findings would be recorded as follows:

1. Price: 22–23
2. Earnings: 1960—$1.24   1961—$2.00
                        (No current period reported)
3. Ratio: 11½ times ($23 ÷ $2)
4. Number of shares outstanding: 860,000
5. Net current asset value per share less long-term debt—$14.43

	Computed as follows:
Current Assets:	20.1 million
Minus Current Liabilities	5.7 million
	──
Minus Long-Term Debt	2.0 million
	──
Net Current Assets	12.4 million

Net current assets (12.4 million) divided by number of shares outstanding (860,000) equals net current asset value per share (less long-term debt).

Conclusions:

1. Price: (price, alone, has slight significance).
2. Earnings: sharp increase of slightly more than 60 per cent.
3. Price earnings at 10: 11½ times earnings looks quite promising for a possible Undervalued if future investigation bears out continuance of earnings improvement.
4. Number of shares outstanding: very thin and stock is traded over the counter. Caution.
5. Net current asset per share less long-term debt: with net current assets approaching the selling price of the stock, the company appears very strong financially.

Conclusion: Standard Screw Corporation looks promising. Further investigation would be in order. The utilization of the "screening" of a stock through the first look requires minimal work with maximum effectiveness. The location and investigation of a stock with as much *"promise"* as Standard Screw Company would lead you into the "second look" at the *potential* Undervalued Stock.

8

The Six Steps of
the Second Stage
of the Investigation

*A detailed explanation is given to provide a clear understanding
of where to look, what to look for, and how to interpret the results.*

THE MERITS OF STATISTICS

The meat and bones of investing profitably is the investigation that precedes purchase or sale. All too often, the review of "dry" statistics is a bore, a painful chore to be performed as quickly as possible—something like gulping distasteful medicine. A great part of the reason for this is that figures are little symbols that conspire against being captured by the imagination in the same way that the romance of products or growth does. It is much more titillating to read of the great strides being made in the aerospace industry; of manned space vehicles drifting at thousands of miles per hour into the unknown of new planets; of the billions of dollars which will be invested to further this exploration; about the thrilling thoughts of not only a new industry but a new technology leading us into a new and wholly different world; of the possible benefits of world-shaking discoveries—all of these are much more exciting than "the amount of working capital available as of the year ending December 31, 1961." Even the language of accounting—the precise, formalized, unyielding phrases of the balance sheet or the income statement—are themselves repelling: "cost of goods sold"; "net tangible assets"; "capital surplus"; "capital structure." It is an arid language lacking color and verve—about as romantic as a black iron frying pan. But that homely frying pan, unchanged for generations, lasted for these many years because it is better for the purpose it fulfills than anything developed since. The weight, shape, and pure functionalism of this pan has served every house-wife well—it is dependable, simple, and practical. So it is with accounting. There comes a point in every investment where the flowing glamour of projected plans, products, and so on, must recede into the shadows, as the cold financial facts are subjected to the harsh glare of investigation. This is the area where there is no room for romance; this is the area where dreams will collide with reality; this is the area of brick and mortar—tangible and real. This is why we do not want romance getting in the way of the facts. There is more to be gained for the investor by starting with the untarnished financial facts than with the rumors of great new breakthroughs or new products. The reason for this is that if the company under consideration does not have the financial means to achieve success, then, barring some exceptions, it will not succeed.

THE SECOND LOOK

The second look at the Undervalued Stock uses this philosophy to alert the investor to financial conditions only, leaving the distracting items of plans and products to a later stage. This look is almost as brief as the first look and its purpose is the same on a little deeper level: to provide additional facts to serve either as an elimination step for the company or to provide further reasons for a more thorough study. There are six steps in the second look as noted:

1. Sales
2. Cost of Goods Sold
3. Gross Profit
4. Cost of Sales
5. Net Profit
6. Book Value (Net Tangible Asset Value per share)

Sources of Information

With the second look, we go to a different source for our information. Whereas the Standard & Poor's Stock Guide served us for the first look, we now go to one of the financial service manuals. For our purposes, we have used Moody's Industrial Manuals. In the second look, the items sought are all contained in the income statement, except for book value, which is computed from the balance sheet.

The income statement is a report which shows what revenues come in and what monies were spent. Like almost all financial statements, it is presented in a comparison form. The 1961 income statement would carry in an adjacent column the comparable totals for the previous year. As in the case of the first look, this is designed as a fast examination, so only the previous two full-year statements are used, as well as whatever limited information is available from current reports. (Quarterly reports are generally quite limited, concentrating only on the main facets of operation.)

FUNCTION OF THE SECOND LOOK

Looking to evaluate the company's operating performance in only the barest outline, the second look provides a measure of what direction sales are tending, what the margins of profit are, and finally what the asset value of the company is. In the second look, it is the directions of sales and profit margins which are the tell-tale indicators of whether to cancel the candidate or pursue it. American Home Products Corporation has been an extremely successful company for many years, but in early 1962 a view of profit margins showed them to be shrinking. The earnings growth rate was slowing and, though growth was continuing, the slowdown in the rate was sufficient to warn the investor investigating the company. Admittedly, the time period of two years makes for a very shallow examination, but it will be sufficient at this level of the investigation.

Though dry figures cannot be romanticized, it may serve to stimulate lively interest to keep constantly in mind that the figures in the company reports may add up to profits or losses in your pocketbook. With this in mind, this and subsequent steps become more dramatic.

Step 1—Sales

Reported as net sales to show the actual amount of dollars received or owed to the corporation by purchasers of its products, this total usually indicates the sole source of income to the corporation. The company enjoying expansion of its markets will often show sizeable gains in sales figures, but, like every other criterion used, sales alone can be misleading. There have been many instances when sales have increased while earnings have declined. Acquisition of competing companies often inflate sales figures for the acquiring corporation very rapidly. If previous sales volume had been $20,000,000 annually and a new company is purchased with sales of $10,000,000, the resulting combined total of $30,000,000 may look like an imposing accomplishment. But, as usual, there are often some overriding considerations that can change this rosy complexion to a pallor. The digestion of acquisitions is often painful. The merging of common operations to effect savings may be long delayed. New lines of authority within the surviving corporation may be blurred, with resulting costly inefficiency. This is intended to point up the fact that sales alone are not absolutes: they are guides.

Sales increases are what the Undervalued investigator looks for. The uptrend in sales is usually the prime requisite for earnings improvement. Without expanding sales, the long-term chances for earnings gains are diminished. Cost-cutting is thoroughly desirable, but cutting costs has a lower limit beyond which a corporation cannot go without impairing its operations.

The fetish for "growth" has been derided and blamed for many of the abuses in the investing arena, whereby prices are driven beyond reasonable limits through overenthusiasm; *but* growth in sales, and hence in earnings, is the strongest armor available to the investor. The static corporation is not a desirable investment medium for more reasons than just earnings. The company, like the individual, which rests on its laurels of former success is wide open to the attrition that must follow complacency. The drive and aggressiveness of management are sapped as the leaders flee the company to use their talents in a more dynamic organization. The always present necessity to take risks is throttled by the defensive hedge of protecting what they have. This defensiveness has toppled empires (national and political empires as well), because the competitive edge is dulled. Opportunities are lost to competitors who will and do enter the risk situations and capitalize on them. Markets are eroded gradually and the defensiveness feeds on itself. The old football adage that "the best defense is a good offense" is as applicable to corporations as it is to nations and football teams.

Sales figures are written as follows:

	1960	1959
Sales	36.4 M	34.9 M

Because sales are merely one block in our construction process, it will be worthwhile to consider them not as absolute but as part of the whole picture. If the sales figures are off sharply, close Moody's Manual and wait for the next signal of the next stock investment candidate. If sales are steady or up only slightly, the subject may be tarnished, but carry through at least the remainder of the second look, for it frequently happens that level earnings may represent a pause rather than an arrest of the growth rate.

The ideal situation is a strong upward movement in the sales figure; and the truly strong situation is one where the other elements in the operating picture are running in the same direction.

Step 2—Cost of Goods Sold

The element of costs is a vital one in the relationship to earnings. For purposes of definition, the accounting practice has been to break down costs into two broad areas: (1) production costs (cost of goods sold); and (2) administrative and distribution costs (costs of sales). The cost of goods sold incorporate all of the elements that go into the cost of producing the product or service of the company. The cost of raw material used in manufacture, the cost of wages for production employees, the cost of equipment used in production, the cost of the plant in which the products are fabricated, the costs of maintenance, taxes, heat, light—all of the costs that are a direct result of manufacture of the product are added together to give a total "cost of goods sold."

The costs of manufacture are generally the greatest expense element in the corporate earnings picture. This is usually the area where profit squeeze or expansion is controlled. An increase in the cost of wages without a consequent rise in prices will result in less net earnings unless savings are effected in another way. The prime use of cost of goods sold to the investor is to give him a picture of how well the company performs its production function. If there is an increase in the cost of cocoa in 1961, and we are examining Hershey chocolate in 1962, we may find that profit margins will vary between the two years (unless they make the chocolate bars smaller, of course). If the cost of goods sold has increased from one year to the next, it will be difficult to judge from dollar totals whether or not this increase represents a deterioration of costs if the sales have also increased. The happy event of improved sales naturally would increase cost of goods sold, but we wish to determine whether or not the company is in a profit squeeze, or whether, in the face of improved sales, it is achieving greater efficiency. This is accomplished by dividing the sales figure into the cost of goods sold to obtain the percentage of sales dollar that cost of goods sold represents.

As an illustration of this, the Western Tablet and Stationery Company (American Stock Exchange) showed the following sales and cost of goods sold totals for the years 1959 and 1960:

	1960	1959
Sales	36.4 Million	34.9 Million
Cost of Goods Sold	31.2 Million	30.6 Million

It is evident that gauging the improvement or decline in these figures on the basis of dollar totals with a sales increase of $1,500,000 is awkward. By reducing cost of goods to a percentage of sales, we have a quick and valid picture of the cost trend. Thus the cost of goods sold is seen as follows:

	1960	1959
Cost of Goods Sold	85.7%	87.6%

The result shown indicates that, in this particular area, Western Tablet receives a plus for reducing their cost of goods sold coupled with a rise in sales. There is much to be said for a company with costs dropping in any instance, but when costs (in these days of spiraling costs) are falling with sales rising, the investor will find good reason for continuing to look at the potential Undervalued.

Here again it is the direction and strength of movement which encourages or discourages further investigation. It will be seen that each element, when added together, will present a substantial springboard for judgement "to buy" or "not to buy."

Step 3—Gross Profit

Gross profit is the number of dollars remaining to the corporation after it has paid for the cost of goods sold.

Using the same illustration of Western Tablet, the gross profit of the company is computed as follows:

	1960	1959
Sales	36.4 Million (100%)	34.9 Million (100%)
Less: Cost of Goods Sold	31.2 Million (85.7%)	30.6 Million (87.6%)
Gross Profit on Sales	5.2 Million (14.3%)	4.3 Million (12.4%)

"Gross" means "fat or bloated," and in the accounting sense this meaning carries through. Gross profit is bloated because only one expense element has been deducted from sales. The reason for using gross profit is to give interested parties a clear view of how well the company performs its production job, without considering any other element. If gross profit is taken as a percentage of sales, we can eliminate the percentile computation used in the preceding step; because cost of goods sold in 1960 was 85.7 per cent of sales, it is evident that the gross profit on sales was 14.3 per cent.

Step 4—Cost of Sales, plus Step 5—Net Profit

These two steps are taken together because the net profit figure is so much a part of the results of the cost of sales that it would be difficult to separate them meaningfully.

Cost of Sales is the second leg of the corporate cost picture. This is where the management must manage very closely, because though production costs account for the largest expenses, management is often restricted in its drive for improvement in this area. Outside forces such as raw material costs (uncontrolled), wage costs that are fixed by contracts, and plant changes or equipment changes that may take years to incorporate, are some of the problems faced in this area. In the cost of sales category are joined all of the expenses necessary to market, advertise, sell, and transport the products as well as the administration costs of running the corporation: the office personnel, sales forces, and executives salaries are all in this cost section, as well as the special promotions, and every miscellaneous expense incurred, down to stamps and stationery and water coolers.*

The cost of sales is the deduction from gross profit which results in net profit. The net profit figure is the ultimate target for the investor, but again costs affect earnings and the investor is very much interested in how well management manages. The cost of sales is another index of efficiency and direction of corporate profits. If, as in the case of Eldon Industries in 1961, management spends a substantial amount of money on an advertising promotion to increase sales, and we find that the sales increase achieved was not sufficient to cover the cost

---

* See Appendix: "Fixed Charges."

of the campaign, we may find that even in the face of rising sales we have declining earnings. The other side of this cost picture is the abuses of corporate money by management. Although not often found in any corporation, it is found occasionally that substantial expenses are incurred through "fringe benefits" such as airplanes, boats, and other "necessary" items in companies, which are not of sufficient size to make such investments anywhere near reasonable. There is no attempt here to deny the need for expenses and expensive investments to improve or increase business, but cost of sales is the best gauge of management efficiency. This fact becomes quite apparent during "lean times" for a business, when management succeeds in lopping many items off its expense rolls and quite effectively tightens its belt. The company which maintains a taut rein on expenses during good and bad times will show higher earnings as a result of this efficiency. Crown Cork and Seal Corporation (NYSE) is a fine example of a company which has achieved a good growth in sales with extremely low increases in costs during this growth.

Because cost of sales is vital in itself, it is used in the same fashion as cost of goods sold—i.e., as a percentile of sales. To learn the consistency of costs, it is compared for the two most recent full-year reports.

Since Western Tablet was used as an example in the previous step, we will use it again.

	1960	1959
1. Sales	36.4 M	34.9 M
2. Less: Cost of Goods Sold	31.2 (85.7%)	30.6 (87.6%)
3. Gross Profit	5.2 (14.3%)	4.3 (12.4%)
4. Less: Cost of Sales	1.6 (4.3%)	1.4 (4.0%)
5. Net Profit	3.6 M (9.9%)	2.9 M (8.3%)

The costs of sales increased three-tenths of 1 per cent on a sales increase of slightly more than 4 per cent.

The control of costs demonstrated in this very brief period is encouraging.

The net profit figure (before taxes) is the amount of money which the corporation earned on its business operations. Net profit is the goal of business and investors. Taking net profit as a percentage of sales, we as investors are given a clearer picture of the "trends" of profits. The often talked about "margin of profit" is what we look for here. Though sales may have increased and net profit also increased, it *may* have been a Pyrrhic victory for management if margins of profit were hurt by the expansion.

Referring again to Western Tablet and Stationery, the net profit in 1959 was 8.3 per cent of sales, while in 1960 it increased to 9.9 per cent of sales. As an index of improvement, this increase in margin coupled with a slight improvement in sales is encouraging. Since earnings are to such a great extent arbiters of price, it is imperative that the indices of earnings power (the first five steps of the second look) be pointing up in order to enhance your profit potential in a stock investment.

The growth factor in stock prices is predicated on the anticipated earnings improvement of the growth company. This has been overdone in some instances and overanticipated in others. The growth rate in International Business Machines has been at a rate of 20 per cent for some years. Even if the rate of growth declines to 15 per cent, it means a 100 per cent improvement in earnings in a little over 7 years. This rate, coupled with many years of proven performance under extremely competent management, has resulted in investors' putting a premium price on the stock for many years. This is understandable, when it is realized that the economy as a whole is growing at a rate of 4 per cent. Confidence in growth, however, can be misplaced. A company which earned 20¢ in 1960 and 40¢ in 1961 certainly has grown substantially; but the other factors of stability, strength, fiscal responsibility, industry outlook and competition would certainly make an investor pause before launching himself into such a situation.

Step 6—"Book" Value (Net Tangible Asset Value per Share)

Leaving the income statement with the completion of the net profit step, we move to the balance sheet to obtain a "safety line" on the company: "book value."

In the days when stocks were valued on asset value, the book value was the most sought-after figure in the company's financial statements. By adding together all of these assets and deducting from this figure a total of all the liabilities, the resulting total is net asset value.

The net asset value (not to be confused with net *current* asset value computed in the first look) is based on total assets (fixed and current) and the excess in value represented by these assets over the total liabilities. As in the case of net current assets, the book value has negligible influence on the price of a stock. It is a safety line to the investor to prevent exposure to the danger of complete failure by a corporation. The evidence of risk in all investments is besieging us daily in our newspapers: the unforeseen and unforeseeable lurks as a constant threat to all investors. A prolonged strike, natural disasters, a revolutionary discovery by a competing firm—these, and hundreds of other events, may jeopardize the formerly rosy prospects of "our" company. To provide some protection against the worst disaster of all—bankruptcy—the investor looks to asset values as a meaure of protection against obliteration.

The added necessity for this protection in companies which have been in the loss column for some years provides the single greatest reason for continued existence of the corporation. With assets, the company may be "worth" more dead than alive, and the assets may provide a floor in the stock price sufficiently lower than the stated value of the assets to allow for the attrition which always occurs under a forced sale.

Curtiss Wright Corporation had a book value of approximately $25.00 per share, and the stock was selling as low as $16.00 per share in 1961. There are many companies on the New York Stock Exchange selling at less than book value. This does not insure that these stocks are necessarily buys. The asset value merely provides the Undervalued investor with the safety measure needed to prevent him from falling into the pit of the undercapitalized speculation. The number of stocks selling for mere pennies is mute evidence of the fact that stocks can go to nothing as well as increase in price. The investor who buys 10,000 shares of a 50¢ stock has bet $5000 on the expectation that this company will survive and prosper. Consolidated New Pacific Limited (American Stock Exchange) in fertilizer, and with a steel rolling mill, is a good example of the toll that is taken of stock prices with a consistently weak performance and a shaky financial base. Selling at a high $2.50 per share in 1961, the stock was selling at 62½¢ in early 1962. Where does it go from there? As long as losses continue, there is only one way—down.

The point to be made is that a company in financial trouble, without adequate financial or credit reserves, loses a tremendous amount of the flexibility and sheer muscle needed to drag itself out of the bog of losses. Asset values provide muscle. The Undervalueds need muscle.*

SUMMARY OF THE SECOND LOOK

After the elimination stage of the first look, dealing largely with surface evaluation of the stock in relation to price, earnings, and a fast test of financial strength with the net current asset value, the second look takes a still tentative but closer look at a few of the operating indices of the company.

Still classified as an elimination phase of the Undervalued Method, the second look provides a short-term (two years) review of some prominent operating figures which enable us to save time and effort by casting aside the company with: (1) declining sales; (2) increasing costs; and (3) narrowing profit margins or weak financial condition represented by poor asset values. Though hard-and-fast rules are always dangerous, especially with stocks, it will be necessary to state that declining sales and narrowing profit margins are two factors which immediately preclude further investigation. Remember that "change" is what

---

* See Appendix: "Liquidity of Assets."

creates incentive for investor activity in stocks and that "change" for the worse will undoubtedly "worsen" prices. Even though earnings have shown substantial improvement, if margins of profit and sales are shrinking, it must follow that earnings will soon follow the same trail.

The Meaning of Margin of Profit

The "margins" used are gross profit and net profit. Declines are dangerous in these areas, but remember also to maintain some perspective. If sales are up sharply and margins have narrowed slightly, do not throw out the stock. In cases of expanding sales, there will very often be excessive costs incurred as management hurriedly fills the gap between old and new demands for personnel, advertising, and so on.

There is always a lurking danger in making flat statements about anything relating to stocks and stock prices. In the case of declining margins of profits and sales, it is not *always* the case that earnings will suffer from such declines, although certainly it is most often the case.

The experience of some corporations in this the heyday of diversification has been that some one segment of the corporation might be losing money while the other divisions are prospering. In such cases, you may see sales up, with earnings and margin of profit down, due to the drag exerted by the losing division. It can happen and has happened that the corporation will divest itself of the losing division and very rapidly return to a strong earnings uptrend. This same experience might be seen in a corporation engaged in one industry but supplying a varied "line" of products to its customers. It sometimes happens that the discontinuance of an unprofitable line of products can produce the same strong result of relieving pressure on earnings.

New plant start-up costs (nonrecurring) will also effect margins in cases where production expansion is underway. As a general rule, if sales are up sharply, then give the benefit of the doubt to management and continue to investigate, providing, of course, that all of the other tests have been passed satisfactorily.

If sales are down, or static, with profit margins down and costs up, discontinue the examination. As regards book value, there must be applied "the uncommon characteristics of common sense" to the evaluation of this element. If a company being reviewed has been losing money for some time and is giving strong evidence of a recovery in profits, then asset value above the current price of the stock will be a prerequisite. The reasoning here is that the unforeseen may occur and the promised earnings might not materialize. If this happens, the protection of asset value is mandatory to prevent complete disintegration of price before you have an opportunity to sell.

Judging the Facts

If, on the other hand, the company has been quite stable in earnings with a consistent record of profitability, the relationship of asset value per share to the price of the stock will not be as stringent as that imposed on the loser. While we are discussing a matter of degree, it must be evident that an arbitrary limit of "75 per cent of selling price," or any other limit, would possibly eliminate many otherwise satisfactory candidates. In lieu of this, let the degree of risk decide the requirements for you. If the company has been erratic in performance, then strong asset value, close to the selling price, would be required. If the company has shown steady improvement in all operating areas, including earnings, assets of less than 50 per cent of selling price will be adequate.

The second look, in the best circumstances, will show a company with sales increasing, costs declining, margins of profit expanding, and a book value double its selling price. Because every company is different, we will encounter wide variations in our tour through the valley of the Undervalueds.

9

A Hard Look at
Performance—
The Final Act

Covered in the same detailed fashion as the first two stages, this chapter takes a hard look at the outline of the final step in the Undervalued Method.

Since our aim is profit through common stocks, it may be worthwhile to start the "third look" with the ancient bromide that "things worth having are worth working for."

Profits are worth a measurable amount, limited in absolutes only by the variations which take place in the value of the dollars so earned. Stocks are measurable also, not in absolute terms, since so many outside forces sway investors' confidence, but by utilizing the "measurable," you are then placed in a much stronger position to take advantage of the facts, and put them to work for you, instead of fighting them.

Harking to the old quotation about work, the third look is a work step. This step requires a deeper and broader look at the company under study. The first two steps were merely scanning devices used to inform you whether or not the company held the "promise" of a change significant enough to afford you a profit opportunity, and the protection necessary to permit you to invest with confidence. Since your dollars will be involved, it will be necessary to probe and dig, evaluate and judge, *before* investing. It bears repeating that these investigations carry no guarantees—only protection and prospects.

THE THIRD LOOK

This step examines a four-year operating record of the company, plus whatever current period reports are available. In most cases, it is desirable to examine a six-to-ten year history of operations, but four years covers the minimum time period consistent with safety and the limits of other demands on our time and energy. Four years permit establishment of trends in all categories, as well as a display of possibly erratic changes. This examination starts with a history of the company. In the financial manuals are concise reviews of a corporation's business. Since, in many instances, examination of little-known companies will be undertaken, this is an especially valuable assist. Heretofore, we have only scanned the surface, but if the company has withstood the first two tests, then it is time to look at what they do to earn their corporate living.

The corporate history contains the date and state of incorporation, a description of the products made, where plants and facilities are located, the number of employees, names and locations of subsidiaries, and pertinent data of particular interest concerning the corporation, including capitalization and capital structure.

The third look repeats several items which have already been examined in the earlier procedures, though in this instance over a longer period of time. The steps involved in the third look are as follows:

1. Working Capital
2. Assets: Total
            Current
            Fixed
3. Liabilities: Current
               Long Term
4. Number of Shares Outstanding
5. Earnings
6. Price Range
7. Price Earnings Ratio
8. Book Value Per Share
9. Sales
10. Cost of Goods Sold
11. Gross Profit
12. Sales and Administrative Expense
13. Net Profit

Step 1—*Working Capital*

If you had an opportunity to buy stock under a stock option plan at a price one-third below the market value of that stock, but were unable to do so because of a lack of funds, then it might be said you were short of working capital.

The same condition holds true for a company. If they can effect savings on purchases of raw material of 2 per cent by paying cash, but are unable to do so because of capital shortage, then they are adding unnecessary and substantial costs to production.

Working capital is the same as net current asset value. The difference between what is owned in cash, marketable securities, inventories and accounts receivable, and what is owed to employees for wages, accounts payable, taxes, power, etc., is net current assets, or working capital.

The degree of flexibility with which management can expand its sales force, hire new personnel, conduct bold new advertising campaigns, will be largely controlled by its working capital position.

The third look seeks to discover, first, if working capital is adequate, and secondly, if it has been growing over a four-year period.

Step 2—*Assets*

The asset side of the balance sheet displays the value of each article of worth which a company owns: the current assets are shown in one section and fixed assets in another. The reason for this breakdown is to enable you to determine what cash resources are available to the company in a reasonably short time, and to display the fixed or not so mobile assets.

There is interest in asset values, but beyond that it is desirable to examine the assets themselves. This is not to say that all of us are to become Hawkshaws, capable of ferreting out overstated values, but to permit judgment to act on what is revealed. Patents and goodwill are generally carried at nominal value of $1.00 by most companies, because it is at best a guess as to their true market value. So if we find a company carrying goodwill at $1,000,000, we would immediately deduct that amount from the asset totals. If there were one million shares outstanding, this would result in a devaluation of one dollar, in both net current asset value per share (less long-term debt), and book value per share.

If inventories are the largest portion of the current asset, while cash and receivables are very small, and if those inventories are of a specialized nature not lending themselves to easy liquidation (heavy equipment, for example), it would be wise to value those inventories at perhaps 50 per cent of stated value for purposes of obtaining a truer picture of the current position of the corporation.*

When strange assets are shown—strange in the sense that they are far afield from the company's primary operations—further investigation may be needed. Although we are in an era of diversification and it is not usual to find a clothing manufacturer in the chemical business, those "foreign" assets may be a danger signal.

Since the possible ramifications of analysis of assets are enormous, it is not intended that everyone become expert on asset valuations. But the asset figure will be quite revealing for the purposes of the Undervalueds. If there is, for instance, a drop in value of current assets of 40 per cent from one year to the next, the question will be raised, why?

If there is no corresponding increase in fixed assets and no operating losses

---

* See Appendix: "Inventories."

to account for this decline, it may then be necessary to take the time to send for the company's annual report. A change in the method of evaluation of inventories may have caused this; or perhaps some old item, formerly carried on the books, was written off as valueless. The point to be made is: find out what happened.

In the fixed asset department are found the company's real estate, plants, and equipment. These are generally shown at cost prices, and included in this section of the balance sheet is a direct deduction from the fixed assets for depreciation. (If this item does not appear on the asset side, where it belongs, then it may be shown as a liability or part of surplus reserve.) Thus the fixed assets are shown at their depreciated value.

Since fixed assets loom large on the books of most businesses when we are examining a "losing company," it will be necessary to adjust mentally the asset values downward to allow for the possibility of forced sale of fixed assets. When a company carries a plant on its books and that plant is old and worn, it is almost a matter of guesswork as to what the market value of the property would be under voluntary or involuntary sale.

The examination of asset values for four years will provide a measure of growth, contraction, or possibly changed direction. Illustrative of the latter case is the trend of recent years for many companies to lease rolling stock, and in some cases real estate and equipment, instead of purchasing. This trend is based on the reasoning that money invested in the operation of the business will yield a better return than that tied up in real estate or trucks, for example. Thus we may find fixed assets declining, while current assets increase (as do current liabilities).*

In this step, each level of the asset side is examined—i.e., a four-year record of the current assets, the fixed assets, and finally total assets.

Step 3—*Liabilities*

A fear-inducing term which seems to thunder is—liabilities are debts. The business of business is to buy (thus incurring an obligation to pay) a material, fabricate it (thus incurring an obligation to pay for the work of fabrication), and sell the fabricated product, thus incurring a right to be paid.

The first steps, however, are to pay, and liabilities is the collective heading under which all debts are shown. Liabilities, like assets, are also in two classes. Long-term obligations are those which a company incurs to finance large capital items—plants, equipment, and so forth. The corporation usually seeks the same type of financing as we do on an individual basis. When purchasing a house, we utilize the house itself as a basis for a long-term loan from the bank. Mortgage loans are a part of long-term debt. Long-term debt in most instances is defined

---

* See Appendix: "Return on Investment Capital."

as extending beyond two years, with fixed increments of repayment involved.

The corporation also has the resource of issuing bonds. Bonds are debt obligations which may take several forms. Mortgage bonds are those issued using the assets of the corporation as collateral for the loan. Debentures are like IOU's, with a much more impressive title. The corporation promises to repay at a fixed date in the future the face value of the bond, and with certain other rights sometimes accorded the lenders, it also agrees to pay a fixed amount of interest at specified times annually. The general credit of the corporation is the basis for offering these debenture bonds.

Convertible bonds are debentures, with the added fillip of enabling the bondholder to convert his bond into a specified number of shares of common stock. The convertible bond is issued to "sweeten" the appeal of the loan, since the bondholder may realize appreciable profits if the price of the stock exceeds the conversion parity price. In the meantime, he has the protection of a bond (debt obligation has precedence over equity rights) and a fixed interest payment.

Long-term debt, as is evident, can take several forms and the interest on this debt is a portion of the company's liability picture.

The general term "liabilities" alludes to all current debts of the company. As previously discussed, these obligations consist generally of bills due currently. The importance of these obligations is in their relationship to assets. A company which has liquid assets (cash and marketable securities) sufficient to meet all or nearly all of its liabilities is incomparably stronger than that company whose assets and liabilities are almost in balance.

Within the liability structure, there are sometimes discovered tell-tale signs of weakness. Short-term bank loans, for instance, may indicate that the company is faced with financial problems. Extensive increases in accounts payable may indicate the corporation is extending itself at the expense of its creditors. The result of this could be higher future costs, as suppliers start to worry about the credit of the company.

Liabilities over the same four-year period will reveal trends of strength and weakness. An examination of the individual items comprising liabilities will draw attention to those showing substantial changes from year to year and cause us to inquire why. The answer to that question may immediately cause us to stop investigation.

Step 4—Number of Shares Outstanding

The reason for incorporating this step in the third look is to provide an accurate look at the changes that have occurred in common stock outstanding. Thus earnings of $8.51 per share in 1957 may make earnings of $2.36 per share in 1960 look as though a terrible decline has occurred unless we find that the base of number of shares has changed. Although most per-share earnings figures for past years are adjusted for splits and dividends, this is not always the case when we are using reference manuals.

Step 5—Earnings

The subject of earnings has been dealt with quite extensively. The ramifications of earnings changes on stock prices is the single greatest influence on this pricing structure. From earnings it will be apparent why a four-year record of the company's history is studied. A two-year trend, as shown in the first look, can be quite misleading, whereas four-year studies can provide some interesting surprises. What may look like a strong recovery on a two-year basis may prove to be a weak one when previous years' earnings are examined.

Step 6—Price Range

How low is low? And when is a stock undervalued? These are questions which can only be answered when the price is related to other yardsticks. The general market climate certainly has an influence on all stock prices, and companies in the same or related industries can also be used as a further measure of relative value. The history of prices paid in the past for the stock by willing investors is one of the strongest indications of what we may expect similarly disposed investors to pay in the future, given the same or similar conditions. If we found that the range in price of a stock in 1957 was $19.00 to $31.00, with earnings of $2.00 per share (10 to 15 times earnings for the year), we could reach some reasonable conclusions. Assume we are examining the same stock in 1961 (four years later) at a price of $6.00 and strong indications that after losing money for two previous years the company appears to be returning to profits of $2.00 per share, we may conclude that investors will *probably* return the price to at least $19.00, or 10 times earnings. We may, on the other hand, find some stocks which have sold during this four-year span at prices which range very narrowly. These instances will help us to form judgment on what type of price pattern we may anticipate in the future *unless* the change we are looking for is so substantial that prospects are good that valuation will change also.

As important as price range is as an index of the future, so is the relationship of price to the multiplier important as examined in step seven.*

Step 7—Price Earnings Ratio

If the range in price one year was $26.00 to $38.00 on earnings of $2.00, we would take the mean price ($32.00) and divide by the earnings ($2.00) to

---

* See Appendix: "Pre-tax & After-tax Earnings."

obtain the average price earnings level of the stock for that year (16 times earnings). If, in the subsequent three years, the average price earnings ratio had been 12 times, 18 times, and 14 times, this would tell us whether our suspect corporation was selling at a depressed level or at a historically high one. The relative value of the stock at the time of examination is the truest index of what can be expected in the future if the earnings condition returns to the high levels achieved in prior years.

Step 8—Book Value per Share

Once a company starts to lose money, creditors of that company become a little nervous. Stockholders become nervous, too, but prospective investors should be even more nervous. Losses are not just per share earnings figures. A loss of $1.00 per share may not mean too much to the casual onlooker, but translate that into 2,000,000 shares and that $1.00 looks awfully imposing.

Where do those losses come from? Who paid out the dollars (2,000,000 of them)? Those dollars come from the corporation; whether from cash, earned surplus, or increased obligations to pay, the net result was and would be a decline in net tangible asset value per share.

The protection feature of asset value is our prime purpose in seeking substantial levels of "book" in relation to price in the Undervalued Stock.

Step 9—Sales

The pivot of every qualifying test of corporate operation is sales. Once a company starts to improve in sales, a momentum is created which puts still further impetus behind the drive. Aggressive selling begets more aggressiveness, and a snowball effect can be achieved. The changes which occur in business earnings and business trends do not occur overnight. Years of preparation, building of organization, product improvements, changes in distribution—each area of change for the better contributes its share to the performance of the whole. It is because trends take time to start and because they tend to accelerate, or at least continue to carry forward at the same rate, that we look very closely at the trend of sales.

Downward trends have the same multiplying effect as upward ones. Consider for example, the plight of the company dealing in a consumer product whose sales start to decline. Management performs fantastic gyrations to stop the slide—special promotions, sales meetings, new distributors, accounts are solicited that have not been approached in years—but to no avail. The slide continues. A spiral is created. Less advertising results in fewer sales, fewer sales result in fewer orders as retailers see the dust mounting on their inventories; sales decline, costs are cut but not fast enough to keep pace, and earnings drop.

The fact that a company's sales are in a downtrend should have been evident from the first or second look. However, sometimes the two-year trend will be up, while over a four-year term it is evident the company's sales are heading down.

Sales which are erratic—up one year, down sharply the next, up slightly the next, and so forth—represent a very dangerous enterprise for the investor. This danger alone makes the four-year review not merely desirable but necessary.

Steps *10 through 13*

The final process in the third look is to gather the all-important four operating statistics, which we have mentioned before. These comprise Step 10—Cost of Goods; Step 11—Gross Profits; Step 12—Cost of Sales; and Step 13—Net Profit.

Because it is so evident that human talent is the most important element in any enterprise, these four steps provide the most telling record of how well management performs. On the financial record is a clean portrait of what has happened and a good indication of what will happen.

The effect of management actions on costs and margins of profit is the ultimate test. When a stock is studied which bears out effective control of costs with rising prices, and margins of profit which are maintained or improved with rising sales over a four-year span, confidence is buoyed and investment becomes desirable, not fear ridden.

SUMMARY OF THE THIRD LOOK

The third look covers a minimum number of facts. It must be understood that these brief steps do not provide an all-inclusive framework of evaluation of the merits of a particular company. There can be, and are, objections to omission of some elements of the corporate structure which are of great importance. Dividends, for example, have an influence in stock prices, yet we have skirted them. Dividends provide a measure of price protection far greater than asset values, yet for the Undervalued Stock, dividends as such are not as vital as knowledge about operations. "Cash flow"* is another statistic much talked about in recent years by many reputable analysts and given considerable weight in evaluation of a company. Cash flow is the amount of net profit earned by the corporation, but with depreciation added back on. The reason for using this figure is to present an uncluttered picture of how much money the company is generating that can be used in furthering the expansion of that company.

---

* See Appendix: "Cash flow."

There are several major items and many minor ones which could have been appended to these steps, but the criteria used have been: (1) safety; (2) operations information and projections.

Investigation before investment is an absolute necessity. The investigation, however, must be kept within reasonable limits of practical application.

By investigating the working capital, assets and liabilities of the corporation, a quantitative test is given to the subject. These are safety requirements. In examining a four-year record of the operating performance of the company through sales, costs, and profit margins, a quantitative test is given to determine if the record is strong enough to warrant your investing your dollars. Projections of what "should" happen are calculated from these facts.

The steps taken are much briefer than they appear to be when accompanied by a text.

The benefits to be reaped by utilizing even such a bare outline as this will be twofold: salvation from entering weak, faltering stocks with probable attendant losses, and protection when entering strong stocks. They must be applied, first, when purchase is effected, and second, as long as the stock is held, so that sale may be effected when a downtrend starts.

10

Protection of Capital and Enhancement of Profit Potential: A Case in Point —McCall Corporation

This is a fairly typical Undervalued Stock and is subjected to the Undervalued Method to demonstrate some interesting methods of making projections in earnings, as well as to demonstrate that the "dull" company which is evidencing a decided change for the better will be honored by the "market" with higher prices.

The element of luck has been credited by many people for their own or someone else's success. There is no disputing the degree to which adverse or propitious events can affect the prices of shares of stock; but over a period of time and through many investments, Lady Luck's influence must give way to the work of facts. Success will be achieved by the knowledgeable. The "guesser" or "hoper" cannot be successful over a long period of time if he is merely stabbing at investments, because the odds against being continuously lucky mount with each new commitment.

Because investors are generally quite bright, and because in time investors will invest in shares of successful companies, it follows as dawn follows night that the key to successful investing must be in the performance of the corporation.

Illustrative of this we shall review through the eyes of a would-be investor the stock of McCall Corporation as it appeared in early 1958. (McCall Corporation is presently traded on the New York Stock Exchange.)

THE SIGNAL

On January 7, 1958, the following signal appeared in the financial press: "Official changes: Herbert Bijur and H. M. Williams have been elected directors, and T. A. Bruinsma appointed Secretary."

As a signal it is not too revealing; it is merely an official change. All that the signal has done is to attract our attention to the stock. The meaning or possible meaning of this change is of little or no importance at this time. It is also not too far beyond imagining that we have never heard of McCall Corporation, and we shall assume for our purposes that nothing is known about the company.

THE FIRST LOOK

Step *1—Price*

The evening paper reveals that McCall Corporation is selling at a price $13.00 bid and $13⅜ asked. (In the event that you have some difficulty remembering the meaning of bid and asked prices, put yourself in the position of an owner of the stock who wants to sell. Ask yourself which price you *think* you'd wind up receiving (not which one you would like to receive) and you will have the answer: the lowest price for a seller (the bid) and the higher price for the buyer (asked).)

Step *2—Earnings*

Going to Standard & Poor's Stock Guide for the rest of the information needed, we descend on the all-important earnings, where the following facts are shown.

Nine months ending September 30, 1957 shows earnings of $1.51 per share against $1.24 per share earned in the first nine months of the previous year.

An earnings increase of 27¢, or almost 22 per cent, is quite impressive and results in heightened interest.

The two previous years' earnings are:

1956	*1955*
$1.16	$1.74

Just from the earnings report, scanty as it is, there are some conclusions that can be drawn.

Nine months' earnings		Full year	
1957	*1956*	*1956*	*1955*
$1.51	$1.24	$1.16	$1.74

The company suffered a sharp decline in 1956, with a reduction of 58¢, or almost one-third of its previous year's earnings.

The nine months' report for the current year indicates a strong recovery is underway. But notice also that, for the first nine months of 1956, the corporation earned $1.24 per share, while for the full year of 1956, earnings were $1.16. Therefore, McCall Corporation *lost* 8¢ per share in the final quarter of the previous year. Since the fourth quarter last year was weak, we might well surmise that the fourth quarter of the current year will perhaps also be weak. This will stop us from "annualizing" the current earnings for nine months of $1.51

per share into $2.00 for the full year (9 months, or 3 quarters, divided into $1.51 indicate earnings of 50¢ per quarter, thus $2.00 for the full year).

Taken in relation to the price of the stock, the earnings shown for the period are strong enough to continue investigating.

Step 3—The Price Earnings Ratio

Using the last full year's earnings (of $1.16 per share earned in 1956) a price earnings ratio of 12 times is determined (13⅜ ÷ $1.16).

This is not too high a price, even considering that in early 1957 the market in general was quite low. But in spite of this ratio of past performance, it is far more important to consider the price of the stock in relation to the current earnings level of the stock.

Since we have seen that the fourth quarter for McCall Corporation is weak, it will be safer to project full-year earnings at the same amount shown for nine months. The reasoning used in this instance is that 22 per cent improvement has been achieved and that this improvement should continue through the fourth quarter, thus permitting the company to operate at least at a break-even point for the period. It is found that the stock at current levels is selling at slightly less than nine times earnings.

Because the price earnings ratio is nebulous and no man can say "this is how much that stock is worth," we seek *relative* guides in this area; and since nine times earnings *appears* reasonable, we are constrained to continue.

Step 4—Number of Shares Outstanding: 610,165

The stock outstanding is very thin, less than three quarters of a million shares, thin enough to warrant caution in buying or selling but not so thin as to restrain us from considering the stock further.

Step 5—Net Current Asset Value per share less long-term debt

In 1958, McCall Corporation showed net current assets for the last full year reported:

	1956	1955
	12.8 M	12.6 M
Less Long-Term Debt	7.5 M	7.5 M
	5.3 M	5.1 M

The dollar total of net current assets less long-term debt is 5.3 million and 5.1 million for each of the years shown. By dividing the number of shares outstanding into these totals, a per share valuation of $8.60 for 1956 and $8.30 for 1955 is indicated.

The financial strength of the company is very encouraging. With the stock priced at 13⅜ showing a current asset position of almost three-quarters of the price of the shares, it provides substantial assurance that we are not dealing with a marginal corporation.

THE FIRST LOOK SUMMARY

1. Price: $13.00–13⅜
2. Earnings:

Nine months ending September 30, 1957		Full year	
1957	1956	1956	1955
$1.51	$1.24	$1.16	$1.74

3. P x E Ratio: 9 X (estimated)   12 X
4. Number of Shares outstanding: 610,165
5. Net Current Asset Value per share less Long-Term Debt:

1956	1955
$8.60 per share	$8.30 per share

The first look has shown a stock selling at a reasonable price with a decided improvement in current earnings (22 per cent) capable of earning a substantial amount (as shown by the $1.74 in 1955) with a few number of shares outstanding. There is a very solid financial base, as shown by the net current asset figures.

No negative factors of sufficient weight have been discovered to divert us from pursuing a potential Undervalued Stock.

THE SECOND LOOK

Because interim period reports are skeletal, the bulk of our material will be obtained from the more detailed annual reports of the most recent two years. However, when available, the bare facts supplied in quarterly reports should be used in conjunction with the year-end figures.

Step 1—Sales

McCall Corporation supplied sales figures for the nine months report and sales were shown as follows:

Nine months ending September 30, 1957		Full year	
1957	*1956*	*1956*	*1955*
51.5 M	46.1 M	60.9 M	53.7 M

It is interesting to review the conclusions derived from the sales figures in relation to what has already been learned from the first look.

Starting with 1955 sales of $53,000,000 and earnings of $1.74 per share, it is with some surprise that we see sales in the following year up over 13 per cent to $60,900,000 and earnings down that year by over 30 per cent to $1.16.

In the current period, sales for the nine months are almost equal to full-year sales for 1955 and have improved sharply by 11 per cent over 1956's already improved sales. Coupled with an obvious improvement in profit margins for the current period, this is a highly encouraging factor.

Step 2—Cost of Goods Sold

Using only the full year's figures, the cost of goods sold is as follows:

1956	*1955*
44.7 M	39.5 M

With the increase in sales, it is not surprising that the dollar total of cost of goods has increased, but it is important to determine how well costs have been managed. In 1955, cost of goods sold accounted for 73.5 per cent of the sales dollars, and in 1956, 73.4 per cent. There is a decline of one-tenth of 1 per cent on improved sales: certainly management has not fallen down in this area of control.

Step 3—The Gross Profit

The McCall Corporation showed a very handsome increase in gross profit in 1956, going from 14.2 M in 1955 to 16.2 M the following year. A 13 per cent increase in sales has resulted in a 14 per cent improvement in gross. It is, much too early to crow, however, since we have seen a disappointing earnings performance in 1956. Since gross profit is the other portion of cost of goods sold, adding up to net sales, we already know the percentage has been very stable: 26.6 per cent in 1956 versus 26.5 per cent in 1955.

Step 4—The Cost of Sales

1956	*1955*
11.8 M (19.4%)	9.7 M (18.1%)

It is apparent that McCall Corporation must spend sizeable sums of money to achieve its sales. In 1955, it took 18.1 per cent of each sales dollar to obtain those sales. Since the cost of goods sold took a sizeable bite of that same dollar, it is already evident that the company operates on a narrow percentage profit.

In 1956, cost of sales had increased from 18.1 per cent to 19.4 per cent. An increase of this size (1.3 per cent) in some industries would perhaps not be too significant, but in this case it probably is.

Step 5—Net Profit

Net profit is profit before taxes, and is used to show more clearly how well the corporation operates before sharing earnings with the silent partner— Uncle Sam.

(It must also be realized that the Undervalued Method has ignored completely the element of depreciation and several other deductions which account for the seeming discrepancy between cost of sales and gross profit results in net profit.) *

The net profit for McCall Corporation is as follows:

Nine Months		Year end	
1957	1956	1956	1955
2.2 M	1.5 M	2.0 M	2.2 M

On 13 per cent higher sales in 1956, the company has earned $200,000 less than what was achieved in 1955.

The percentage of profit in 1955 was 4.2 per cent of sales, while in 1956 it was 3.4 per cent. This narrowing of margin would in many instances be sufficient cause to discontinue investigating the stock even if earnings had improved on increased sales. This would be especially true of a company whose margins were narrow to start with. In this instance, the benefit of current period net is available for further comparison of the trend of net profit. It is found that the net profit for the first nine months of 1956 is identical to the results achieved for the full year 1956 (3.4 per cent). In the first nine months of 1957, net profit margins improved to 4.4 per cent, bettering those achieved in the best year reviewed to date (1955, with 4.2 per cent).

Since there is some evidence available that current period earnings are consistent for the full year (1956 net for nine months of 3.4 per cent exactly equaled full-year net of 3.4 per cent), it is possible to make some projections. Granted that we are using the rather thin reed of one previous year's performance as the prop for our projection, it is nonetheless not unreasonable to assume that continuance of a trend over a relatively short span of three months is probable.

---

* See Appendix: "Fixed Charges, etc."

Since sales for the nine months are up 11 per cent over the sales made in the same period of the previous year, we may make our projection as follows:

Assuming this sales rate continues for the full year, we may take 11 per cent of 1956 sales (6.7 M) and arrive at a sales total for 1957 (6.7 M + 60.9 M) of $67,600,000.

As the net profit before taxes is running at a current rate of 4.4 per cent of sales, we may compute total net at 2.97 million. Allowing 50 per cent for tax payment (the corporate tax rate is 52 per cent of net earnings over $25,000), we arrive at an estimated $1,480,000.

With 610,196 shares outstanding, it is indicated that per share earnings *could* be $2.40 per share.

Our earlier evidence of a lagging fourth quarter in the previous year tempers the hot excitement of a huge projected improvement in earnings, *but* there is sufficient evidence of substantial improvement to provide *reasonable* hope of continued improvement for the full year. The greatest ground for this hope is provided by the improved margin of profit.

Step 6—Book Value

McCall Corporation shows surprising strength in net tangible asset value per share.

1956	1955
35.56	49.51

Shown also is a substantial decline in asset value of almost $14.00 per share in a one-year period. The company had not lost money in the years noted, and if assets had been sold (unless at figures ridiculously lower than the book valuation), there would not have been any substantial reduction. The safest assumption is that obsolete assets had been written off the books to a true reflection of their real value: worthless.

This decline can be investigated, but for our immediate purposes the aim of determining the fiscal strength of the company has been achieved. A book value almost triple the price of the stock gives reasonable assurance that McCall Corporation will not suddenly go broke.

THE SECOND LOOK SUMMARY

	Nine Months		Full year	
	1957	1956	1956	1955
Sales	51.5 M	46.1 M	60.9 M	53.7 M
Cost of Goods Sold	—	—	44.7 M	39.5 M
			(73.4%)	(73.5%)

	1957	1956	1956	1955
Gross Profit	—	—	26.2 M	14.2 M
			(26.6%)	(26.5%)
Cost of Sales	—	—	11.8 M	9.7 M
			(19.4%)	(18.1%)
Net Profit	2.2 M	1.5 M	2.0 M	2.2 M
	(4.4%)	(3.4%)	(3.4%)	(4.2%)
Book Value Per Share			$35.56	$49.51

Sales have been climbing at an impressive rate and the improvement seems to be continuing through the current year. One of the greatest single elements required for growth in earnings is improved sales.

Cost of goods sold has remained constant for the two years, which is encouraging in the face of the sales improvement.

The increase in cost of sales is a disturbing element in this second look, and one which in most instances could be accepted as a necessary corollary of improved sales. However, the narrowness of margins of profit adds greater significance to even small increases in this cost area.

As stated earlier, net profit would have cast serious doubts on the advantage of continuing the investigation if the current period figures were not available to demonstrate the "turn around" in the downtrend started in 1956. The return to a level of 4.4 per cent in 1957 from 3.4 per cent the previous year provides excellent reason for discounting 1956 results and going forward with the examination.

The book value of $35.00 per share adds greater confidence to this stock, and provides the qualitative degree of safety needed to make an investment if the third look bears out the indications gained through the first two steps.

The McCall Corporation has presented substantial evidence of being an Undervalued Stock. The third look is in order and there is no reason to delay the investigation of the longer-term performance record of the corporation.

THE THIRD LOOK

A brief history of the company reads as follows:

"History: Incorporated in Delaware February 6, 1913, to have perpetual existence. Acquired capital stock of the McCall Corporation (incorporated in New York in 1893) which was outgrowth of pattern business established in 1870 by James McCall. First number of *McCall's Magazine* was issued September 1897.

"On July 31, 1929, acquired all the publishing assets of the Consolidated Magazine Corporation, an Illinois Corporation publishing monthly magazines: *The Red Book* and *The Blue Book*, in consideration of 25,603 shares of common stock. New Publishing Co. (Del.) was organized to publish these magazines.

"On November 1, 1936, dissolved the operating companies: The McCall Company and the New Publishing Company.

"Magazine Photo Engraving Corporation, a wholly owned subsidiary, was liquidated at close of 1950. Business is now operated as a division.

"Business and Products: Company prints and publishes magazines and produces under contract magazine products of other publishers.

"Company Publications: *McCall's Magazine*
        Redbook Magazine
        McCall's Pattern Book
        McCall's Dressmaking Book
        McCall's Needlework Patterns Catalogue
        McCall's
        McCall's Today

"The Company produces magazines under contract, including: engraving, composition, making of electro type, as well as high-speed color presswork, and binding. Service also includes mailing of subscription copies. Company produced for itself and others more than 768 million magazines and patterns in 1956, an average of about 3 million magazines and patterns each regular working day.

"Magazines printed under contract include: *Newsweek, Christian Herald, Popular Science Monthly, Progressive Farmer, Mademoiselle, U.S. News and World Report, Reader's Digest, Air Force, Elks, Catholic Messenger, Outdoor Life, Charm, Electricity,* and the *Farm Scholarship*."

Step 1—*Working Capital*

Computed on a per-share basis by obtaining the net current asset value (current assets less current liabilities divided by the number of shares outstanding), the following record was shown by McCall Corporation in January of 1958:

| | Nine Months Ending September 30 | | Full Year | | | |
	1957	1956	1956	1955	1954	1953
Working Capital	$21.82	$20.02	$21.93	$22.31	$21.78	$24.08

McCall Corporation has working capital of impressive size in relation to the price of the stock.

Step 2—*Assets*

Current: A review of the current assets reveals a steady improvement over the 4¾ year period (except for the slight dip in 1956 due to writedown of goodwill and mailing lists).

Fixed: The steady improvement from 1953 through 1955 was sharply arrested in 1956.

Assets:	Nine Months		Full Year			
	1957	1956	1956	1955	1954	1953
Current	20.2 M	16.5 M	17.1 M	18.0 M	14.0 M	13.2 M
Fixed	—	—	16.3 M	25.0 M	23.1 M	22.4 M
Total	—	—	33.4 M	43.1 M	37.9 M	35.7 M

In periods of rising sales, it is axiomatic that current assets rise as accounts receivable increase on the basis of the increased sales. Inventories must also be larger to take care of increased production demands. The decline in current assets in 1956 in the face of improved sales is an anomaly which could be attributed to improved inventory controls combined with tighter collection procedure. This is, at best, conjecture. Using the period of time involved to determine a trend, the asset picture is one that is moving up. The strong improvement in 1957 is heartening and the absence of erratic changes over the full four years is equally encouraging.

Step 3—Liabilities

	Nine Months		Full Year			
	1957	1956	1956	1955	1954	1953
Current	6.9 M	4.3 M	4.3 M	5.4 M	3.9 M	5.2 M
Long Term	—	—	7.5 M	7.5 M	3.1 M	1.7 M
			11.8 M	12.9 M	7.0 M	6.9 M

Since current liabilities tend in the directions of sales, it is not surprising to see the increase in these obligations until—again the exception—a decline takes place in 1956. The sizeable advance in 1957 is more in the order of a "natural" result of the sales improvement. Noting again the absence of sharply erratic performance, the current liabilities are weighed and found acceptable.

In the case of long-term liabilities, the company has increased these obligations substantially since 1953. The debt is almost covered twice by net current assets, so there is sufficient margin of safety to allay latent fears.

Step 4—Shares Outstanding

Nine Months		Full Year			
1957	1956	1956	1955	1954	1953
610,196	610,196	610,196	610,196	610,196	610,196

No change in the number of shares outstanding in the period under review.

Step 5—Total Earnings

	Nine Months			Full Year		
	1957	1956	1956	1955	1954	1953
	922,886	806,600	705,365	1,061,812	1,334,835	1,174,921

Earnings Per Share

Nine Months			Full Year		
1957	1956	1956	1955	1954	1953
$1.51	$1.24	$1.16	$1.74	$2.19	$1.93

Step 6—Price Range

Nine Months			Full Year		
1957	1956	1956	1955	1954	1953
17¼–12½	25–12⅞	25–12⅞	25½–20⅝	23⅞–15	24¼–15

If earnings are the final determinant of where prices go, the record of price range is the single greatest valuation measurement the investor can obtain.

In the situation with McCall Corporation, a four-year low price of 12½ (1957) and a high of 25½ (1955) provides immediate evidence that the current price (13⅜) is near enough to the old low to provide sufficient room for substantial gains *if* the stock follows its former pattern.

Step 7—Price Earnings Ratio

Though the price range of a stock is a good index of value, it is more effective to relate price earnings and obtain a mean P.E. ratio for each of the years under review.

P. E. Ratio: Nine Months			Full Year		
1957	1956	1956	1955	1954	1953
10 X	16 X	16 X	13 X	9 X	9 X

The low price earnings average of 1953 and 1954 was improved to 13 times on reduced earnings and maintained at steady levels on even lower earnings in 1956, resulting in a higher rate of valuation. It is apparent that the effect of a two-year decline in earnings was not fully reflected in the price of the stock until 1957.

At 10 times earnings, the seeker of Undervalued Stocks is again given additional grounds for expecting improvement in the price earnings ratio *if* earnings improvements can be maintained.

Step 8—Net Tangible Assets Value Per Share (Book Value)

Nine Months			Full Year		
1957	1956	1956	1955	1954	1953
—	—	$35.56	$49.51	$50.69	$47.05

Step 9—Sales

Nine Months		Full Year			
1957	1956	1956	1955	1954	1953
+11%	—	+13%	+9%	+5%	—
51.5 M	46.1 M	60.9 M	53.7 M	49.3 M	47.0 M

The point of "trends" has been belabored throughout the exposition of the Undervalued Method. It is and has been emphasized because a "trend," once established, carries momentum in the direction of the trend. The longer that the trend (up or down) has existed, the greater its momentum. In terms of investment, the owner of the shares in a company which is trending up can continue to hold his shares until the flattening-out signs appear. In the case of McCall Corporation, the upward trend of sales is encouraging in that it is consistent and fairly substantial.

Step 10—Cost of Goods Sold; and Step 11—Gross Profit

	Full Year			
	1956	1955	1954	1953
Cost of Goods Sold	44.7 M	39.5 M	36.4 M	35.0 M
	(73.4%)	(73.5%)	(73.8%)	(74.6%)
Gross Profit	16.2 M	14.2 M	12.9 M	11.9 M
	(26.6%)	(26.5%)	(26.2%)	(25.4%)

For all practical purposes, it is the consistency of percentage of sales represented by cost of goods sold which is most pertinent in this review. By relating past performance of cost control to the future, there is provided a measure of confidence (or distrust as the case may be) in the future if the previous years have been controlled within a narrow range. Imagine the risks inherent in investing in a company characterized by erratic fluctuations in cost of goods sold. Ranges of 15 or 20 per cent, variations from year to year, can only represent risk to an investor—i.e., that "his" year of purchase will be one of low costs. By determining the level of costs, it is at least possible to determine what may be expected in the future from what has occurred in the past. McCall Corporation, over the four-year period, has displayed a very consistent cost of goods sold level.

Step 12—Cost of Sales

Full Year			
1956	1955	1954	1953
11.8 M (19.4%)	9.7 M (18.1%)	7.7 M (15.7%)	7.3 M (15.7%)

Like the successful businessman using his new-won affluence to indulge in longer lunches and higher-calory dinners, resulting in a larger belt-line, corporations often do the same thing.

McCall Corporation has grown fat around the middle of its sales and administrative expenses. Perhaps expense accounts are not watched so carefully, or extra personnel have been hired who are not carrying their equitable share of the sales volume. Whatever the cause, it is evident that management has a problem. Increased cost of sales of almost 4 per cent in a company that operates on a 3 to 4 per cent profit margin means that, had management restrained expenses, earnings would have doubled.

This is by far the most significant weakness yet uncovered in the examination, and it is to weigh in the conclusions made following completion of the third look.

Step 13—Net Profit

Nine Months		Full Year			
1957	1956	1956	1955	1954	1953
2.2 M	1.5 M	2.0 M	2.2 M	2.7 M	2.4 M
(4.4%)	(3.4%)	(3.4%)	(4.2%)	(5.5%)	(5.2%)

Ignoring the dollar totals shown and concentrating on percentage of sales represented by net profit, we are treated to the spectacle of a company which hit a peak percentage in 1954 of 5.5 per cent, followed by a decline to 4.2 per cent in 1955 (when cost of sales increased substantially). Suffering a further decline in the net profit during 1956 to 3.4 per cent, we see a reversal of the decline that took place in 1957, when nine months' earnings were running at a rate of 4.4 per cent. It is this reversal which is most important at this juncture. A company with improvement in sales and a decline in earnings has evidently taken the steps necessary to *start* resurrecting the levels attained in 1953 and 1954. A promising element and one of the key determinants for judgment, the net profit margin improvement in the current period is a large plus in favor of the McCall Corporation.

THE THIRD LOOK SUMMARY

Marked by substantial earnings in 1953 and 1954, a drop of almost 50 per cent has taken place a scant two years later, in 1956. The attrition in earnings (which occurred in the face of rising sales) may serve as an object lesson of the fallacy of remaining in securities whose earnings are declining. The stock had fallen to a four-year low in 1957, providing an apparent opportunity to take advantage of a *change* in the direction of earnings as evidenced by the recovery in the first nine months of 1957.

		Nine Months 1957	Nine Months 1956
1.	Working Capital	$21.82	$21.02
2.	*Assets:*		
	Current	$20.2 M	$16.5 M
	Fixed	—	—
	Total	—	—
3.	*Liabilities:*		
	Current	$ 6.9 M	$ 4.3 M
	Long Term	—	—
	Total	—	—
4.	Shares Outstanding	610,196	610,196
5.	Total Earnings	922,886	806,600
	Earnings Per Share	$ 1.51	$ 1.24
6.	Price Range	17¼–12½	25–12⅞
7.	P.E. Ratio	10 X	16 X
8.	Book Value	—	—
9.	Sales	$51.5 M (100%)	$46.1 M (100%)
10.	Cost of Goods	—	—
11.	Gross Profit	—	—
12.	Cost of Sales	—	—
13.	Net Profit	$ 2.2 M (4.4%)	$ 1.5 M (3.4%)

Full Year

	1956	1955	1954	1953
1.	$21.93	$22.31	$21.78	$24.08
2.	$17.1 M	$18.0 M	$14.0 M	$13.2 M
	16.3 M	25.0 M	23.8 M	22.4 M
	33.4 M	43.1 M	37.9 M	35.7 M
3.	$ 4.3 M	$ 5.4 M	$ 3.9 M	$ 5.2 M
	7.5 M	7.5 M	3.1 M	1.7 M
	11.8 M	12.9 M	7.0 M	6.9 M
4.	610,196	610,196	610,196	610,196
5.	705,365	1,061,812	1,334,835	1,174,921
	$ 1.16	$ 1.74	$ 2.19	$ 1.93
6.	25–12⅞	25½–20⅞	23⅞–15	21¼–15
7.	16 X	13 X	9 X	9 X
8.	$35.56	$49.51	$50.69	$47.05
9.	$60.9 M (100%)	$53.7 M (100%)	$49.3 M (100%)	$47.0 M (100%)
10.	44.7 M (73.4%)	39.5 M (73.5%)	36.4 M (73.8%)	35.0 M (74.6%)
11.	16.2 M (26.6%)	14.2 M (26.5%)	12.9 M (26.2%)	11.9 M (25.4%)
12.	11.8 M (19.4%)	9.7 M (18.1%)	7.7 M (15.7%)	7.3 M (15.7%)
13.	2.0 M (3.4%)	2.2 M (4.2%)	2.7 M (5.5%)	2.4 M (5.2 %)

It is not the decline (a change which predictably would affect stock prices), but the improvement in current earnings which feeds our expectations of continued improvement. The *change* in earnings from $1.16 for the full year of 1956 to $1.51 for the first nine months of 1957 is a change of sizeable proportions and one which holds strong promise of change for the better in the stock price.

The facts learned about the company showed a substantial working capital position which provided all the liquidity needed for foreseeable needs as far as the investor was concerned. The asset position showed up extremely well, with a very healthy $35.00 per share in asset value and net assets less long term debt of almost $9.00 a share. These underlying values provide the peace of mind so essential in entering or contemplating investment in a corporation with declining earnings, or an unknown corporation. The liabilities are sufficiently well covered by asset values to preclude concern about them. The additional fact of reasonable control of liabilities with rising sales is an added strong point.

The steady improvement in sales adds lustre to the stock, and evident continuance of this favorable trend leads to the conclusion that participation in this growth will prove profitable if margins of profit improve.

Although cost of goods sold and gross profit are so well controlled as to appear frozen, the steady worsening of cost of sales constitutes the single serious drawback to investing. However, net profit for 1957 has rebounded substantially. The 1 per cent improvement in net profit *indicates* (not proves— just indicates) that management has started to effect the necessary cure for this weakness. This improvement is substantial enough to cause us to overlook previous sins.

The range of the price of stock has given us a good indication that, if earnings continue to improve, investors will be willing to pay up to $25.00 per share. As the lowest price in four years has been 12½ per share, we are in a position to buy near the low, during a period of change for the better, which enhances the profit potential of the stock and our investment dollar. The fact that the current earnings ratio is slightly less than nine times, and that this ratio was last seen in 1954, gives the added edge of a very low price in relation to earnings during a period when earnings are improving.

CONCLUSION

Based on the current earnings of McCall Corporation, the altered trend of profit margins, the continued improvement in sales, the strong asset position, the low price-earnings ratio, the low price in relation to "price history" of the four years examined, and the absence of any overriding fundamental weakness, this stock would qualify as an Undervalued investment candidate. The purchase would be made.

RESULTS

The earnings for the full year of 1957 were $1.84 per share (adjusted for a 3 per cent stock dividend issued that year). In the second look, we engaged in the game of projecting sales and earnings based on facts known for a current period. We projected sales of 67.6 million, based on an 11 per cent increase for nine months over the previous period. Actual sales for the year 1957 were 68.4 million. Our further projection of earnings of $2.40 per share was predicated on continuance of a 4.4 per cent margin of profit. Actual earnings of $1.84 (adjusted) fell substantially below this as actual profit margin for the full year was 3.8 per cent (a much smaller improvement than indicated, but still an improvement over the 3.4 per cent of 1956).

In 1958, the stock rose to a price of $25.00 per share and earnings rose to $2.00 per share. The following year, a small decline in profit margins occurred as the stock rose to a peak of $40.00 per share on news of a three-for-two stock split. By the end of 1960, profit margins declined from 3.6 per cent to 2.1 per cent, and it is reasonable to expect that the Undervalued investor would have taken this as a sure signal to sell. The price level of sale would have been somewhere between $30.00 and $40.00.

In addition to the shrinking profit margin, a historically high price earnings level of 20 times was achieved at $40.00. These two factors, hopefully, would have induced you to flee with a purseful of money—money realized by using facts to formulate your investment program. This was not an overnight profit; it was a long term, and it was sound.

II

"Losers Can Pay"
An Examination of
American Motors

You do not have to be a mental giant to make reasonable decisions based on facts. American Motors should prove to be an eye-opener as a demonstration of what the "trend" of performance can mean to the investor who takes the time and effort needed to read the performance record. American Motors was an extremely interesting Undervalued.

The subject of this section is American Motors Corporation. The time is early 1958, when the following public announcement was made by the management of American Motors (Symbol AMO, New York Stock Exchange).

> "Company plans to renegotiate revolving credit agreement with 27 banks, due to expire 9/30/58, so as to allow for dividend payments."

The date of this announcement was February 25, 1958.

Although many signals are at best obscure, the tenor of the signal itself in this instance is mildly encouraging. The fact that 27 banks were evidently willing to lay out their depositors' money to enable a corporation to make dividend payments is in itself a confidence-building factor for an investor.

The signal given in February would have sent the Undervalued seeker to the first look at AMO.

THE FIRST LOOK

Step 1—Price

The price of the stock at that time was 8⅝. The importance of the price alone has caused a great many investors to lose money that should not have been risked. There is a bargain instinct in all of us: it is often very tempting to buy a stock "because it is down from a high 80 to 24." It may be even more of a bargain at 12. There were many cases of this happening in stocks which had suffered serious reverses and subsequent declines in price in 1962. It is very desirable to buy bargains, but if earnings and profit margins of the stock examined are continually down, the bargain will prove very expensive.

A little time spent investigating will tell you fairly well how much of a "bargain" you are getting. The price alone is not of too much value; but as a guide as to whether you can afford to buy 10 shares or 100 shares, it is of consuming importance. So far, American Motors is only a low-priced stock.

Step 2—Earnings

The first three months show earnings of 88¢ versus a deficit of 53¢. The full-year earnings of American Motors show a deficit of $2.12 (1957) per share and an even more sizeable loss of $3.48 in 1956.

The earnings recovery, as shown in the first quarter (American Motors is on a fiscal year accounting system with their year ending September 30), is extremely dramatic. Because the automobile industry has historically enjoyed its highest sales and earnings in the spring of the year, it is very encouraging to see such strong earnings in the winter, or new-car introduction months. It is, of course, extremely disheartening to see such heavy losses in preceding years, but continuance of the investigation is very definitely called for.

Step 3—Price Earnings Ratio

With losses in the two previous years' operations, the investor is denied the yardstick of price-to-earnings ratio.

The projections of earnings for the full year 1958, based on the first quarter's operations, could be $3.62 (4 x 88¢). However, since conservative estimates are much more in order and projections based on one quarter's performance may be misleading, it will be a hesitant $3.00 per share (estimated), with a resultant multiplier of slightly less than three times earnings. It is not often that price-earnings ratios as low as this are seen, but very often corporations that have suffered long periods of losses will remain at low-price relations to earnings when recovery starts to occur. It is as though seasoned investors who had witnessed the long declines were rubbing their eyes in disbelief at the audacity of this "loser" becoming a winner, and the natural fear that the "recovery" is false.

Step 4—Number of Shares Outstanding

There should be no shortage of stock available for purchase in this corporation, which indicates 5,587,934 shares outstanding.

Step 5—Net Current Asset Value Per Share Less Long-Term Debt

The sizable losses shown by the company in the previous two years lend greater importance to the underpinning offered by assets.

The computation of net current asset value is shown as follows:

Current Assets	$118.0 M
Less: Current Liabilities	71.8 M
Net Current Assets	46.2 M
Less: Long-Term Debt	13.0 M
Net Current Assets less Long-Term Debt	$33.2 M

$33.2 M divided by $5.5 M shares outstanding = $6.00 per share.

The first quality test for American Motors has given evidence of sufficiently strong financial condition to move us onward in the quest for value.

The first look has shown a not untypical case of a company that is seemingly recovering from a period of sustained and substantial losses and moving into very promising earnings. (Because there is always the danger that a false start accounts for the surge in earnings improvement, it is too rash to assume from so cursory an examination that the company is really starting back strong.)

The American Motors Corporation has shown a dramatic improvement in earnings, a low price in relation to those earnings, and a reasonably strong current asset position.

THE FIRST LOOK SUMMARY

Price (February 25, 1958): 8⅝
Earnings:

Three Months Ending			
December 30, 1957		*Full Year*	
1957	*1956*	*1957*	*1956*
$0.88	$0.53*	$2.12*	$3.48*

---

* Deficit.

PE ratio:—three times on projected earnings of $3.00
Number of shares outstanding: 5,587,934
Net current assets value per share less long-term debt $6.00

THE SECOND LOOK

Step 1—*Sales*

Quarterly sales for the period ending December 30, 1957 were up 33½ per cent over the preceding years.

Full-year sales for 1957 had declined 11.3 per cent from the level achieved in 1956.

It is possible, from the quarterly sales reported, to make a projection of full-year sales. Working back to the theory of "momentum," whereby a trend once started will *in most instances* continue, we may take the percentage of increase achieved in the quarter (33.5 per cent) and apply that to the full year (1957) sales of $362.2 million. The resultant projected sales are $483.5 million.

Keeping constantly in mind that projections are far from accurate, it is still desirable to utilize them, because the danger of being wrong can be somewhat mitigated by following closely the reported sales and operating margins in the next quarterly report. Thus, if the next report shows an over-all increase in sales of only 22 per cent our projection would be revised; and if any action is indicated by the change, it could be effected.

Step 2—Cost of Goods Sold

On a decline in sales, it is always to be hoped that cost of goods sold will decline also. In a heavy-goods manufacturing industry, this is often a difficult goal. But in the case of American Motors in the year 1957, cost of goods sold as a percentage of sales was cut to 89.2 per cent from 92.3 per cent in the previous year.

Because we are dealing with a company suffering from losses in the period under review, it becomes especially important to look very closely at cost trends. The negative (highly negative) factor of losses needs strong medicine to overcome the danger of reversion to greater losses. It is therefore to some extent encouraging to see a reduction in the greatest expense items in the corporation.

Step 3—Gross Profit

Gross profit improved from 7.7 per cent to 10.8 per cent in 1957.

	1957	1956
Sales	362.2 M	408.4 M
Cost of Goods	323.0 M (89.2%)	377.1 M (92.3%)
Gross Profit	39.2 M (10.8%)	31.3 M (7.7%)

The fact that the corporation improved its percentage of gross profit is encouraging; but even more so is the fact that an improvement in dollar totals of almost $6,000,000 (or about 25 per cent) was brought about on a decline in sales of 11.6 per cent.

Step 4—Cost of Sales

The effective steps taken in the manufacturing area that succeeded in reducing costs have been equally well applied to administrative and sales expenses. Whereas in 1956 cost of sales accounted for 12.4 per cent of every sales dollar (again on lower sales), these expenses were cut to 11.3 per cent in 1957.

	1957	1956
Cost of Sales	41.0 M (11.3%)	50.5 M (12.4 %)

A reduction of $9,500,000 is very impressive, especially in view of the sales increase gained in the first quarter of fiscal 1958. The danger always present in sizeable reductions of expenses in the sales area is that promotion and advertising cutbacks will result in fewer sales.

It is sometimes too tempting to "read into" facts uncovered through investigation the meaning that will permit execution of "buy orders" based on the very shallow merit of one-quarter results.

It is, however, equally rash to be overconservative and to permit the existence of losses to blind you to opportunities when cost reductions of sizeable proportions coincide with sales increases.

Step 5—Net Profit (Loss)

The net profit on sales in the first quarter of fiscal year 1958 ending December 30, 1957, was 4.948 million (as a percentage of sales, 4.2 per cent). This is the only profit shown in the period covered in the second book.

The full-period figures were:

	Three Months		Full Year	
	1958	1957	1957	1956
Net Profit:	4.9 M	2.99 M*	10.1 M*	30.5 M
	(4.2%)	(3.4%)	(2.8%)	(7.5%)

* Deficit

The percentage of loss shown in the first quarter of 1957 (3.4 per cent) had been shorn to 2.8 per cent for the full year. The loss of 7.5 per cent in 1956, amounting to over $30,500,000, was reduced very sharply on fewer sales in 1957. The very substantial trend of *reduction of losses* is a key to successful investing in the potential Undervalued.

If, for example, you had examined American Motors during 1957 when these improvements were showing, it would have been a natural candidate for inclusion in the "future watch list" of stocks. It will often happen that signals will appear in a stock when it is much too soon to buy but when evidence of substantial improvements is at hand. This evidence will perhaps make it desirable to make a note of your findings and await the next report from the company to see if promise has become reality.

Step 6—Book Value (Net Tangible Asset Value Per Share)

1957	1956
$19.86	$21.94

With the stock selling at $8.62½ per share, there is adequate asset value to remove any fears of imminent danger.

SECOND LOOK SUMMARY

	Three Months		Full Year	
	1958	1957	1957	1956
Sales	118.6 M	88.9 M	362.2 M	408.4 M
Cost of Goods	—	—	323.0 M	377.1 M
			(89.2%)	(92.3%)
Gross Profit	—	—	39.2 M	31.3 M
			(10.8%)	(7.7%)
Cost of Sales	—	—	41.0 M	50.5 M
			(11.3%)	(12.4%)
Net Profit	4.948 M	2.994 M	10.1 M*	30.5 M*
	(4.2%)	(3.4%)	(2.8%)	(7.5%)

* Deficit

Book Value			$19.86	$21.94

In the review of sales based on a first-quarter increase of 33.5 per cent, a projection of sales to $483,500,000 was made.

Using the first-quarter net profit margin of 4.2 per cent on these sales, we obtain a projected net profit of $20,000,000.

Based on the number of shares outstanding (5.5 million) projected earnings of $3.62 per share may be estimated for the full year 1958.

This projection is possible of accomplishment. It is not an absolute by any means. The projection serves as a guide to what we may obtain over the remainder of the year.

This projection is a valuable result of the second look, but no less valuable is the discovery of effective and substantial cost reduction in the production and administrative areas.

The reduction of losses from $30,000,000 to slightly more than $10,000,-000 lends a great deal of credibility to the high profits shown in the current report. Added to the "reduction factor" is the fact that these results were achieved on much lower sales.

The final note in the second look was a happy one. Assets of almost $20.00 a share, or nearly two-and-a-half times the selling price, is an element of added encouragement to continue investigating American Motors Corporation.

THE THIRD LOOK

Step 1—Working Capital

1957	1956	1955	1954
$8.27	$9.63	$11.01	$18.92

A decline in four years of over 50 per cent of available working capital shows the deadly effect of losses. As far as the Undervalued investor is concerned, the decline in net current assets (working capital) in an industry requiring large amounts of capital for model changes is a definite negative factor.

If, indeed, the indicated sales are a false recovery, the future of American Motors will be very cloudy. The attrition in working capital adds an element of added risks.

Step 2—*Assets*

The entire balance sheet of American Motors is scarred by losses sustained over the preceding years.

	1957	1956	1955	1954
Current Assets	118.0 M	140.7 M	164.7 M	169.8 M
Fixed Assets	78.0 M	84.2 M	95.6 M	96.9 M
Total Assets	196.0 M	224.9 M	260.3 M	266.7 M

The decline in current assets is to be expected on declining sales. The slow drop from 1954 to 1955 became accelerated in the two near term years, dropping almost $25,000,000 in 1956 and $22,000,000 in 1957.

The drop in fixed assets is largely the result of depreciation charges against machinery and plant during a period when capital expenditure for new equipment was evidently nil.

Step 3—*Liabilities*

A drop in liabilities has followed the drop in sales. Long-term liabilities have remained fairly level. Current liabilities are covered by current assets by slightly more than one-and-one-half times.

	1957	1956	1955	1954
Current Liabilities	71.8 M	86.1 M	102.3 M	87.8 M
Fixed Liabilities	13.0 M	14.6 M	14.0 M	16.0 M
Total Liabilities	84.8 M	100.7 M	116.3 M	103.8 M

The brief review of the balance sheet of American Motors displays consistent drops in both areas of assets and liabilities. As a fairly typical Undervalued candidate, this attrition is not unexpected. It would, however, be sufficient grounds for discounting the investigation if the current assets were less than current liabilities (the acid test).

Step 4—*Shares Outstanding*

Three Months		Full Year			
1958	1957	1957	1956	1955	1954
5,588 M	5,670 M	5,588 M	5,670 M	5,670 M	4,340 M

It is unusual to see even a small reduction in the number of shares out-standing, as is the case with American Motors in 1957. (Reduced by 82,000 shares, it is possible that the corporation repurchased these shares and classified them as treasury stocks.)

Step 5—Earnings Per Share

Three Months			Full Year		
1958	1957	1957	1956	1955	1954
$0.88	$0.53 *	$2.12 *	$3.48 *	$1.23 *	$1.95 *
Total Earnings					
4.9 M	2.99 M	11.8 M	19.7 M	7.0 M	11.0 M

* Deficit

Once more, it is the trend of direction which overrides the amounts of loss. The record sales year of 1955 saw losses of $1.23. In 1956, with costs and sales down, losses almost tripled. In 1957, on lower sales, management started the belt tightening: costs were cut, so that on even fewer sales, losses were down from $19,700,000 to $11,800,000.

Step 6—Price Ranges

Three Months			Full Year		
1958	1957	1957	1956	1955	1954
8⅝	—	8½–5¼	8⅞–5¼	13⅜–8½	14¾–9¾

Having examined the history of the operations of this company for a four-year span, it is interesting to see how investors had evaluated the stock during this period of losses—steady losses.

In 1954 and 1955, the range in price was almost the same. The boom years for auto sales evidently kept hopes up that losses would be turned into profits. When hopes were dealt a severe blow by the losses of 1956, the stock dropped as low as 5¼, reaching a high of 8⅞. (Here again is another example of stocks responding to earnings—or lack of them.) The purchaser of shares in 1954 at a price of 12 or better, who decided to "wait out this bad news," was sitting with dead investment monies during a four-year period of bull movement in the stock market, as investors let American Motors lie dormant through 1955 and then sent it tumbling down in 1956 as losses continued and grew. In 1957, with losses continuing but declining, the same effect was seen as American Motors lay painfully within the same narrow range. This is a good story of the how and why of price movements following performance.

Step 7—Price Earnings Ratio

With nothing but losses for the four years, we have no measure available to guide us for the current price of the stock (8⅝) to the projected earnings of $3.74, in which case the stock is selling at 2¼ projected earnings. Granting the projection may not work out, the stock was currently selling at less than eight times reported first-quarter earnings.

Step 8—Net Tangible Asset Value Per Share (Book Value)

	Full Year		
1957	1956	1955	1954
$19.86	$21.94	$25.39	$37.53

Although bloodied badly, there was some healthy muscle still remaining in the corporate "corpus" of American Motors as 1958 began.

Step 9—Sales

Three Months			Full Year		
1958	1957	1957	1956	1955	1954
118.6 M	88.9 M	362.2 M	408.4 M	441.1 M	400.3 M

Although the sales increased from 1954 to 1955 by about 10 per cent, the downhill slide which started in 1956 lasted two years: 33 million in 1956 and 46.2 million in 1957.

The improvement in sales for the first quarter of fiscal 1958 is the single bright spot in this record. The size of the improvement lends believability to the fact that more than just a shallow recovery is in prospect.

Step 10—Cost of Goods Sold; and Step 11—Gross Profit

When investigating a company which, we are hopeful, is emerging from the red into the black, it is important that the operating sections of the investigation be closely examined. The only basis for profit in our investment is that earnings will be realized. When the balance-sheet items reveal declines, it is possible to accept these as a natural result of losses incurred. However, if the evidence in cost and profit margins lies in the direction of no improvement in these costs, it will represent a danger signal that can be ignored only at the peril of your investment dollars.

Cost of goods sold as it looked in early 1958:

	Full Year			
	1957	1956	1955	1954
Cost of Goods Sold	323.0 M	377.1 M	396.0 M	363.4 M
	(89.2%)	(92.3%)	(89.8%)	(90.8%)
Gross Profit	39.2 M	31.3 M	45.1 M	36.9 M
	(10.8%)	(7.7%)	(10.2%)	(9.2%)

The lowest dollar cost of goods sold was in 1957 on the lowest sales total in the period. More important, however, is the fact that cost of goods sold as a percentage of sales was reduced 3.1 per cent to 89.2 per cent, which was the lowest level achieved in the four-year span.

Gross profit for the same year (1957) was also at the highest point. A 10.8 per cent gross profit percentage is encouraging, but the dollar totals in this instance are even more revealing: $23,000,000 more were gained on $38,000,000 less in sales than what was obtained in 1954.

Step 12—Cost of Sales

	Full Year		
1957	1956	1955	1954
41.0 M (11.3%)	50.5 M (12.4%)	54.1 M (12.3%)	48.3 M (12.1%)

The pattern of cost-cutting is somewhat sharper in the areas of cost of goods sold, whereas the variable "cost of sales" fluctuated with the sales totals. It is only in 1957 that a reduction of any substantial size was made in this latter area. In the three preceding years, the percentage of variation was three-tenths of 1 per cent, while in the most recent, full-year costs were cut by 1.1 per cent.

Step 13—Net Profit (Loss)

American Motors has been ranging widely in its percentage of loss each year. The figures were as follows:

Three Months			Full Year		
1958	1957	1957	1956	1955	1954
4.9 M	2.9 M*	10.1 M*	30.5 M*	19.5 M*	22.0 M*
(4.2%)	(3.4%)	(2.8%)	(7.5%)	(4.4%)	(5.5%)

_____

* Deficit

Losses were suffered in the year with the highest sales (1955)—merely proving you cannot really "make it up on volume"—indicating strongly that costs were far from being closely controlled. It cost American Motors $1.07½ to obtain $1.00 sales in 1956.

In 1957, the premium paid by the company to capture that same dollar of sales was reduced from .07½¢ to .028¢.

It is this evidence of cost reduction and net loss decrease which is the bedrock of confidence for the investor going into a stock purchase of a "loser."

The sizable amount of dollars realized in net profit for the first quarter ($4,900,000) is a gleaming example of a successful drive by a company to come from behind and finish strong. Although a long way from finishing, some evidence of recovery is on hand: 4.2 per cent profit margin on higher sales.

THE THIRD LOOK SUMMARY

		Three Months 1958	Three Months 1957
1.	Working Capital	—	—
2.	*Assets:*		
	Current	—	—
	Fixed	—	—
	Total	—	—
3.	*Liabilities:*		
	Current	—	—
	Long Term	—	—
	Total	—	—
4.	Shares Outstanding	5,588 M	5,670 M
5.	Total Earnings	4.9 M	2.9 M*
	Earnings per share	.88¢	.53¢ *
6.	Price Range	8⅝	—
7.	P.E. Ratio	2¼ X	—
8.	Book Value	—	—
9.	Sales	118.6 M (100%)	88.9 M (100%)
10.	Cost of Goods	—	—
11.	Gross Profit	—	—
12.	Cost of Sales	—	—
13.	Net Profit	4.9 M (4.2%)	2.9 M (3.4%)*

	1957	1956	1955	1954
1.	$ 8.27	$ 9.63	$ 11.01	$ 18.92
2.	$118.0 M	$140.7 M	$164.7 M	$169.8 M
	78.0 M	84.2 M	95.6 M	96.9 M
	196.0 M	224.9 M	260.3 M	266.7 M
3.	$ 71.8 M	$ 86.1 M	$102.3 M	$ 87.8 M
	13.0 M	14.6 M	14.0 M	16.0 M
	84.8 M	100.7 M	116.3 M	103.8 M
4.	5,588 M	5,670 M	5,670 M	4,340 M
5.	11.8 M*	19.7 M*	7.0 M*	11.0 M*
	$ 2.12*	$ 3.48*	$ 1.23*	$ 1.95*
6.	8½–5¼	8⅞–5¼	13⅜–8½	14¾–9¾
7.	—	—	—	—
8.	$ 19.86	$ 21.94	$ 25.39	$ 37.53
9.	362.2 M (100%)	408.4 M (100%)	441.1 M (100%)	400.3 M (100%)
10.	323.0 M (89.2%)	377.1 M (92.3%)	396.0 M (89.8%)	363.4 M (90.8%)
11.	39.2 M (10.8%)	31.3 M (7.7%)	45.1 M (10.2%)	36.9 M (9.2%)
12.	41.0 M (11.3%)	50.5 M (12.4%)	54.1 M (12.3%)	48.3 M (12.1%)
13.	10.1 M (2.8%)*	30.5 M (7.5%)*	19.5 M (4.4%)*	22.0 M (5.5%)*

* Deficit

CONCLUSIONS

American Motors Corporation qualified as a potential Undervalued and purchase would have been made in early 1958 at or near the price of 8⅝.

The company reviewed has been found thrashing about in the depths of steady and severe losses for each of the four preceding years.

All assets have declined, as depreciation charges ate up the value of capital assets and current assets declined in the face of sinking sales.

Working capital was cut more than 50 per cent in four years, from nearly $19.00 per share to a bare $8.27. The survival of the company may be dependent on these sums, so if help is not close at hand, a few more years of attrition may make American Motors a "has-been" corporation.

Liabilities have also declined over the four-year span, and the brightest spot discovered in this area is that they do not exceed assets yet.

A jump of 33 per cent in first-quarter sales—the item which appeared in the second look and so buoyed up interest—is the greatest single factor weighing in favor of investing. Auto sales get their spur from new models, and this company has leaped out smartly in the always critical first quarter (fall and early winter) of the new model year. The previous four-year record is dismal.

American Motors, to the interested investigator in 1958, was far from being a sure thing, but the elements visible to the public were strong enough to indicate that the odds were all in favor of a strong comeback in earnings, and a sizeable appreciation in the stock's price.

RESULTS

For the full year 1958, American Motors showed sales of $470,300,000. Whereas the first quarter showed a profit margin of 4.2 per cent, the full year's results improved this figure to 5.4 per cent. Earnings of $25,300,000 were realized, or slightly less than $5.00 a share. (Note that a substantial tax-loss carry forward exists for this company and that the earnings shown are in effect pre-tax. Therefore, to make them comparable to taxpaying corporations, they should be mentally adjusted to approximately one-half the amount indicated.)

The stock rose steadily in price through the year 1958, until, in 1959, it reached $90.00 a share. At $75.00, the company announced a three-for-one stock split. In 1959, earnings went to $10.69 per share ($3.39 adjusted for the three-to-one stock split) on margins which increased to over 11 per cent.

In January of 1960, the first-quarter report for the three months ending December 30, 1959, showed earnings of $1.19 per share against the previous year's $1.60. With a 42 per cent decline in earnings, realizing the trend was very likely reversing itself, this would have triggered a strong incentive to sell. The price in January 1960 ranged between 25 and 30 per share (75 and 90 pre-split price).

The most impressive reason for making a judgment to buy the stock lies in the area of costs. Reduction of production and sales expense by substantial margins indicate the heightened effect which even a modest increase in sales would have on earnings. An over-all reduction in cost of goods sold of 3.1 per cent in a heavy-goods manufacturing industry where these costs represent 90¢ of the expense dollar is indeed significant.

The net earnings of 88¢ for the period is the spur to buy, not to wait. Weighing the risk in the investment, it will be considered that sales could dry up in the second quarter (not too likely, but a close check on progress can be maintained because auto sales and production figures are published every 30 days, and in the trade publications every 10 days).

The facts of strong asset protection well above the purchase price of the stock, as well as the "signal" that indicated financing arrengements to renew dividend payments, would have and should have provided a reasonable "floor" under the 8⅝ price level.

Thus the American Motors situation has all of the necessary elements for the "loss type" Undervalued Stock, i.e.: (1) a long history of losses, which has served to depress the price of the shares well under the asset values, down close to the net current asset level; (2) a reduction of costs as management effectively pares down the fat in operations; (3) significant improvement in sales, and signs or realization, of a *strong* recovery in earnings.

Assuming that the lowest price was obtained (it usually is, by most of us fallible mortals) long-term profits would have been $5,600 on an investment of approximately $900.

Fantastic? Unbelievable? No—as you have seen it is possible to evaluate through investigation.

You cannot hope to find all of the potential Undervalued Stocks in any given year, but unless you look and check, you will not find any.

12

Two Undervalueds

Containing summary reviews of two Undervalued Stocks, this section covers one which, "at its high," gave strong evidence that it was a buy: such is the story of Singer Manufacturing.

Aldens is a mail order company, which gives us the growth issue as an Undervalued, a short history of what happened, and holds some good lessons on what to look for.

In this chapter are two stocks which are fairly representative of additional examples of Undervalueds. In the last section of the chapter, the statistical summaries of each of these stocks is shown.

SINGER MANUFACTURING (SMF NEW YORK STOCK EXCHANGE)

In May of 1960, Singer Manufacturing was selling at a price of $59.00 per share. At that time, the stock was traded on the American Stock Exchange. Singer is one of the most famous and one of the oldest names in American industry. The Singer Sewing Machine was a much sought-after item when grandmother was a girl. (Who can forget the muttered expletives when grandma's foot slipped off the old iron gate foot treadle?) The signal that focused attention on the stock was a report on foreign sales expansions by the company. The report indicated substantial sales gains in parts of Europe and new plants in the Middle East, Argentina, and Africa.

THE FIRST LOOK

Acting on the signal in May of 1960, you would have found earnings for 1959 at $4.12 per share against 1958 earnings of $2.71. An earnings increase of 52 per cent is not to be ignored, especially when coupled with an encouraging signal indicating further expansion. At a price of $59.00, the stock was selling at 13 times earnings, which on the face of it is not too high to rule out serious consideration. Looking to the asset position, you would have found net current asset value per share, less long term debt, of $66.37 per share.

THE SECOND LOOK

On the first look, this stock seemed extremely interesting. It was a well-known company in a consumer-based industry, affording all the necessary ingredients to spur further investigation. With sales up only 11 per cent in

1959, it is necessary to look at profit margins to determine why earnings had climbed so sharply. The answer lies in a sharp improvement in net profit from 5 per cent of sales in 1958 to 7.2 per cent of sales in 1959. This is perhaps one of the best indices of strength that exist. You will find, in many instances, that margin of profit constitutes the prime factor swaying judgment to buy or sell a stock. In many cases, the improved margins are a forerunner of improved earnings and the converse is true of declines. The percentage of net profit is also invaluable for helping to arrive at an estimate of earnings.

A book value of $92.04 per share, up from $89.75 in 1958, puts the seal of good quality on this stock. With over $60.00 in net current assets and over $90.00 in net tangible assets, the Singer Manufacturing Company appears to have necessary financial muscle to continue to expand.

THE THIRD LOOK

The third look at Singer reveals a very healthy working capital position. In the asset section (from 1956 through 1959), there is an increase of $78,000,-000, the bulk of this in current assets.

Liabilities increased during this period also, by 33 million, or less than half the increase in assets. The relationship of current assets to current liabilities is almost 5.5-to-1 (current ratio), a phenomenally strong showing.

Operating Indicators

The long-term debt is extremely small in relation to the over-all asset picture. In 1957, sales declined by $5,300,000, but the trend since then had been up quite sharply, getting to almost a half a billion dollars in 1959 (496 M). In this area of the operating section of the examination, the most fascinating part is the area of cost and margins. In 1956, cost of goods sold and cost of sales ate up 89.1 per cent of the sales dollars, leaving a very impressive 9.4 per cent operating net profit. But in 1957 (the year, also, of lower sales), costs climbed to 93.7 per cent, and the net was chopped to a far less exhilarating 5.9 per cent. This uninspiring performance continued into 1958, when costs again rose, this time to a flat 95 per cent, dropping the profit margin to a round 5.0 per cent. And since this decline of "only 4.4 per cent" in two years represented "only $19,600,-00" in earnings *not earned* on sales in 1958, some idea of the importance of profit margins can be gained. In 1959, a vigorous improvement is seen as costs are cut to 92.8 per cent of sales (and sales increased 11 per cent), leaving a margin of 7.2 per cent. The strong reversal of the down-trend in operating margin is—when taking all other facts into consideration—the most encouraging sign yet witnessed. (All of the above percentages are pre-tax.)

Price and Earnings

Scanning the price range of the stocks over the four-year period, we find that 33⅝ to 46¾ in 1956 set the pattern of prices for the next two years. The lowest price for the three years 1956–1958 was $31.00, while the highest was 49¾. In 1959, the price ranged from 45¾ to 59½.

The mean, or average, price earnings of the stock for the four years was 9 times in 1956, 10 times in 1957, 15 times in 1958, and 13 times in 1959. The stock held its price very well during the years of declining profit margins. It had not sold at a high multiple of earnings during these years, and the price, though substantial, was nevertheless steady. Notice the effect in 1959 of increased sales and improved margins. The stock had an average price increase of 12 points. Singer Manufacturing has presented quite an arresting portrait. The signal announcing improved foreign sales and more extensive foreign expansion has been backed up in very strong fashion by performance and asset values. Selling at slightly more than 13 times earnings, with a very sharp increase in the earnings figures, the stock looked attractive. With sales growing at a substantial pace and asset values almost twice the selling price, the promise of further improvements is substantial. The final impetus to buy this stock is found in the improved margin of profit.

Conclusions and Results

It has been mentioned that many investors will not "buy at the high." Singer Manufacturing would have been purchased in May of 1960 at a price of $59.00. Singer earned $4.44 per share in 1960 and $5.53 in 1961, indicating earnings of over $6.00 per share in 1962 and selling at $115 per share; the "sell" signal for Singer Manufacturing had not appeared as of this writing.

ALDENS INC.

Some companies must spend huge amounts of capital to provide the equipment and plants necessary to process or manufacture their products. These companies are usually the basic industries. Those industries which provide the basic tools or raw products needed to make the tools for industry—steel, autos, aluminum, coppers, heavy equipment manufacturers—all fall into this high capital category. Other companies that provide an easement, or facility for distribution, or a service, are not required to lay out such huge sums. These companies can, and often do, manage to make substantial amounts of money on relatively small capital. One such company is Aldens.

BACKGROUND

Aldens is a mail order house, which, by means of catalogue service, solicits mail orders for merchandise kept in inventory or on order from manufacturers.

In 1954, the company had earned $3.38 per share, but in the two succeeding years earnings had declined to $2.72, and then to $2.19, for a drop of 43 per cent in two years.

March of 1958 saw an announcement by Aldens that it planned to open 10 new catalogue offices in National Tea Company supermarkets in the Chicago area. The announcement further stated that five experimental offices, half the size of the planned new ones, indicated they would show a profit in the second year, though catalogue stores are generally unprofitable until the third year.

THE FIRST LOOK

With this signal blazing the trail, Aldens would have been found at a price of 18⅞ at the time. The 1957 full-year's earnings were found to be $2.49, up 13 per cent over the previous year's $2.19. Selling at eight times earnings, there would have been sufficient interest to move on in the investigation of this company.

With net current assets (less long-term debt) of $25.77 per share, and slightly more than half-a-million shares outstanding, Aldens seemingly had merit.

The signal in this case has some influence, just as it did in Singer Manufacturing: *expansion of earnings*. The *facts* of already improved earnings (up 13 per cent), coupled with a sizable net asset position, indicates the company is not expanding for survival but for growth, and that it has the funds to do so.

THE SECOND LOOK

Aldens sales increased by $10,000,000 from 1954 through 1957, or slightly more than 10 per cent. This is far from a sensational rate of growth, but the direction of earnings has swung about and an almost steady rise in sales— there was decline in 1955—offers encouragement.

As is often the case, however, it is the operating performance of the company that exerts the greatest influence on judgment.

In 1954, Aldens earned 3.83 per share on sales of 92.4 million. This performance was achieved on a profit margin of 4.2 per cent. The following two years' profit margins declined to 3.4 and 3.7 per cent respectively. (There were only 355,000 shares outstanding in 1954, against 586,000 in 1956; thus earnings for 1954, adjusted to reflect the increase on shares, would have been $2.56 per share.)

THE THIRD LOOK

The percentage of net increased to 4.4 per cent in 1957—the highest percentage achieved in the four years under review.

The price-range of the stock has been from a low of 16⅜ (1957) to a high of 28⅝ (1955). At the current price of 18⅞, the stock is selling near a four-year low.

The average price earnings ratio was 5 times in 1954, 6 times in 1955, 11 times in 1956, and 8 times in 1957. At 7 times earnings, the stock did not look too rich at the time of the study.

Aldens had a book value of $35.49 per share, or about twice the selling price of the shares. This asset protection adds the final umbrella to what appears to be a promising situation.

CONCLUSIONS AND RESULTS

With few negative factors, Aldens in early 1958 offered something more than promise. The facts of substantially improved earnings, coupled with an improved margin of profit, offered a tangible handhold for the investor.

The company operated at the retail level through mail order sales and was moving forward with a seemingly aggressive expansion campaign.

The price of the stock was near enough to a four-year low in price to afford reasonable expectation of improvement in price. The book value—and, in fact, net current asset value—was strong enough to remove any immediate fears of devastating reverses.

The strongest single point, however, is again the improvement in margins. Cost reductions in cost of goods sold is a very healthy sign of good management: Aldens appears to have it.

The judgment on Aldens would have been: buy.

The purchase of Aldens in March of 1958 would have required some patience. Six months later, the price of Aldens was approximately the same as your purchase price.

Earnings for the full year 1958 were $2.91 per share, with profit margins improving to 4.9 per cent over 1957's 4.4 per cent. The price of the stock started to climb and it climbed to impressive levels of almost $90.00 per share. You continued to hold the stock through 1959 and through 1960, because margins of profit and sales were steadily improving.

In the early part of 1961, Aldens reported $2.09 vs. $2.07 per share for 1960—adjusted earnings for stock dividends issued in January 1959 (2 per cent) and January 1960 (3 per cent). This flattening in earnings would have precipitated sale of the stock. The stock declined in the early part of 1961 from $80.00 to $62.00 per share. Assuming reasonable good fortune, a selling price of $70.00 might have been realized.

Aldens was a substantial company with good earnings and showing strong signs of improvement. The price in relation to earnings and the improved margins allowed reasonable grounds for a favorable decision. The action in price of the stock subsequent to the purchase was excellent, in that investors recognized the earnings and earnings potential of Aldens by bidding the price of the stock up to a level four times higher than the purchase price.

THE ADVANTAGES OF UNDERVALUED STOCKS

The "Undervalued" stocks utilized in this and preceding chapters were introduced to demonstrate that corporations are not given to hiding their accomplishments—nor their failures.

By investigating intelligently—not brilliantly, not as a professional—it is highly likely that stocks of good corporations may now and in the future be purchased, with reasonable grounds for expectation of improvement in earnings and equally reasonable expectations of improvement in price.

13

On Selling

A presentation of the major factors affecting the sale of a stock and a résumé of the use of the Undervalued Method in making selling decisions.

The pursuit of profit through equity investments is characterized by tremendous concentration on "what to buy." This book is dedicated to the precept that buying good values will result in profits. But there is a corollary to buying which is of equal importance in the profit picture—selling.

The successful investor is one who puts as much thought and effort into selling as he does into buying.

If you have invested in stocks you are taking risks. The incentive for taking risks is profit. If you have not been profiting from your investments during the greatest bull market in history, there is something wrong with what you are, or have been, doing. Possibly the fault lies not only in what you buy, but, more to the point, in what you have not sold.

This chapter is on selling stocks. It is neither intended nor possible to cover all of the contingencies that may create selling situations. The intention is to point up the prime reasons for selling.

YOU AND YOUR SELLING ATTITUDE

Many people look upon stocks as a "gamble." They look at daily price changes and think to themselves, "If only I were on the 'inside,' so I could participate in these gains." Many people have said, "If I could sit all day like you and watch the 'tape,' then I could make a lot of money." The attitude so often represented is that "one of these days lightning will strike my stocks and they will rocket up in price."

Because of these misconceptions, many investors entrench themselves in weak stocks that grow weaker, and then, with a melancholy shrug, sit docilely by waiting for the lightning to strike so they can "get even."

The stock market is not a casino. Stocks do not move in price because a lucky number is pulled out of a hat. Watching the tape is fascinating, but usually all you will get is tired eyes. Lightning does strike some stocks in the form of sudden, surprising news that alters the earnings outlook of the company. But building your investments on the hope of lightning striking is like building your financial security on the hope of winning the Irish Sweepstakes. As for being on the "inside," there is not much doubt that knowledge of what is going to happen would be helpful, but even "insiders" do not know: they use judgment of present facts to project what will "probably" happen. Fortunately for all of us, we can do the same thing.

Hope versus Reality

The investor must deal with realities, not hopes. If a stock he owns has failed to perform well, he must look to the reasons for the poor performance. If the investor persists in maintaining his position in "losing stocks," he is denying the very reason for taking risks in the first place, i.e., profits. The unfortunate part of keeping weak stocks is that losses are twofold: the weak stock can and often does get weaker, thus creating greater losses of capital, while the available strong stocks rise more. It is little short of ridiculous to keep such stocks, using the rationale that "I cannot take a loss." The loss already exists, yet the fiction persists that it really will not exist until the stock is sold.

This is comparable to some of the political fictions we have been invited to imbibe, such as that "the Chinese Communists are really agrarian reformers." For investors, such delusions about stocks are as perilous to their survival as political fictions are perilous to national survival. The reason is that we avoid the painful infection, we refuse to face realities—and stocks are realities. They move for real, sound reasons.

The Damage from Fear

One other consideration in selling requires some attention: fear. There is no question that all of us would like to sell at the "high." But, to be realistic, very few can or do. There is a great fear of selling a stock because you are afraid it might go up in price after you sell it. This is certainly possible. In fact, it is probable. Fractional or other more sizable jumps in price may occur; but if you know what and why you are selling, the chances are good that your reasoning will prove you right in the future performance of the stock. Do not let greed dictate to reason. If a stock is providing sound reasons for you to sell, by what stretch of the imagination can you envision the same stock providing solid grounds for other investors to buy it? In short, do not discount the intelligence of your fellow investor.

SELLING ON THE FUNDAMENTALS

The concept of buying stocks covered in this book is predicated on the earnings performance of the corporation. It has been demonstrated that, once purchase has been made, it is necessary to continue to watch the performance of the corporation. It is, in fact, more necessary to follow performance *after* purchase, because now you have dollars invested in that performance. It is estimated that two years is the time needed for the fairly typical Undervalued Stock to come to fruition, and it often happens that you will remain in the stock much longer.

The reason for staying with an Undervalued lies in the earnings performance. If you think in terms of buying a corporation (instead of in terms of buying a stock), the buying and selling decisions will in most instances be made for you.

Under the protection of the fundamental "performance indicators" of the corporation, you are provided with the strongest lifelines to profits that are available. The Undervalued Method of Investigation provides a realistic, effective way of pointing you in the direction of the corporation that is evidencing strong earnings improvement.

The Undervalued Method can and does provide an equally strong tool to direct you to *sell*.

Because the price performance of the stock will reflect the earnings performance of the corporation, the investor will relate his *selling decisions* to the *earnings indicators* of the corporation.

THE EARNINGS INDICATORS

The operating figures of the corporation are the reports on which the investor leans for making judgments. The first five steps in the second look are the backbone of the operating statement of the corporation. The steps:

> Sales
> Cost of Goods Sold
> Gross Profit
> Cost of Sales
> Net Profit

By examining the corporation whose stock you hold against these five steps each time an earnings report is issued, you will have a reasonably valid indicator of the *trend* of performance in earnings.

Theory of Momentum in Selling

It must be recalled that the validity of these earnings indicators lies in the fact that *trends* in business do not usually change direction very quickly. The "Theory of Momentum," covered at some length in the Undervalued Method, indicates strongly that when a corporation starts to slide in sales or in costs (and therefore in earnings), it is not usually the case that such a slide is quickly reversed. Because of this fact of the *validity of trends,* it is a reasonably safe assumption for the investor to conclude that flattened or declining sales will not dramatically recover in the second quarter if the first quarter sales are down. So, too, if net profit is down from the previous period, it is safe to assume that management cannot, in a three-months period, cut costs quickly or sufficiently deep to reverse the trend of margins of profit. Since declines carry the seeds of further declines, just as growth contains its own stimulus for further growth, the investor can reasonably and profitably pin his sell decisions on the operation of the corporation.

It is, therefore, not only earnings, but, more importantly, the indicators of earnings that can and do provide the reasons for selling.

It is the precept of the Undervalued Method that "change" in earnings direction is the cornerstone of profits; so, too, it is "change" in the direction of earnings which is the signal to realize those profits, or sadly to take a loss.

It is obvious that the first three steps of the first look—price; earnings; price earnings ratio—will be a constant part of every investor's review of his stocks. When the earnings report is made, the combination of the first five steps of the second look (the operating review), coupled with the price earnings and price earnings ratio, will provide an adequate and indeed an effective signpost to sell or hold.

Interim Reports

Often the corporation's interim statement only reports sales, net profit, and earnings, omitting cost of goods sold, gross profit, and cost of sales.

The benefit to the investor lies in the value of even this limited information, as for example, sales of the XYZ Corp. were up slightly more than 7 per cent, earnings were down from 64¢ to 28¢ and net profit was off from 6 per cent to 3.5 per cent.

The value of the operating and earnings figures for the corporation lies in their pointing out the trend of performance. The investor who is guided by the corporation, not the stock, will be in a position to make money.

To provide a hard-and-fast set of rules for all stocks in all markets is not possible, but it is possible to provide a solid framework for selling decisions using reasoned judgment of corporate performance.

Though it was stated at the beginning of this chapter that it was not possible to cover all the "contingencies" possible in a selling situation, it is well to note several major factors that are often present in many stocks and which affect the "fundamentals."

The quarterly or interim earnings reports for many corporations reflect the seasonal nature of that corporation's earnings. Retail stores such as Macy's will show their strongest earnings in the fourth calendar quarter, when the impact of Christmas shopping sends sales up sharply. Many other types of corporations have these same seasonal fluctuations. The seasonal nature of earnings does not detract from the merits or value of using these interim reports as indices of what is to come. The *percentage* change and the *direction* of movement in a weak seasonal quarter will still provide a valid basis for projecting earnings for the full year, unless a nonrecurring element has caused the change.

It must be seen that quarterly earnings, standing alone, can be misleading, whereas quarterly earnings compared to the same quarter of the previous year, and these results in turn compared to previous full-year earnings, will provide a good picture of what might be anticipated for the full current year.

Industry Trends

A further consideration in the "fundamentals" approach to security evaluation, which has not been covered in the Undervalued Method, is that of "Industry Trends."

It is wise to keep abreast of the over-all trend for the general industry in which your stock operates. It sometimes happens that a stock becomes a sale candidate, not because of fundamental weakness in the corporation itself, but because of weakening of the entire industry. When adversity strikes an industry, as can and does happen (witness steel, and savings and loan stocks in 1962), then the reason for sale moves outside the corporation and would be based on the reason for the adversity in the industry itself. The importance of this selling reason cannot be overstressed. If the industry outlook becomes bleak, and there is reason to believe that the actual or anticipated adversity will or might affect earnings or earnings improvement, a valid sell signal will have been provided.

The fundamentals provide the cornerstone for selling decisions as well as buying decisions. A review of the general types of stock price/earnings performance can serve to illustrate the benefits of putting the fundamentals to work for your own profit.

THE FLAT STOCK

Aside from the Undervalued Stock, the fundamentals of every stock will tell you what your chances are for gains or losses. Many stocks are indecisive in their performance direction. All cases will not be clear-cut selling situations. Fortunately, most situations will describe from their profit-and-loss statements what you may anticipate, because of the *fact* that *stock prices will follow the earnings trend of the corporation*. If earnings are flat and likely to continue flat, then the price of the stock will remain relatively stable. If this type of stock is selling at a reasonable price to earnings ratio in comparison with similar companies in the same industry, your vulnerability to sharp declines is not too great. It should be clearly realized that the longer the period of unchanged earnings lasts, the lower the price of the stock will probably go. The reason for this is the natural attrition which takes place as bored investors tire of waiting for price improvement and start to sell their stocks. Buyers, or potential buyers, on the other hand, are discouraged from entering the situation because of the uninspiring corporate performance, thus setting the stage for selling pressures to outweigh buying pressure.

This type of situation is only a "sell" because it lacks potential for gains, and this should be sufficient cause to abandon the stock. How do you know the stock will not suddenly come to life?

Because stock prices follow earnings, and if earnings are flat, the price will almost invariably remain flat. If sales are relatively unchanged and margins of profit are basically unchanged, you have two key elements that indicate flat performance continuing. This situation would call for a thorough review of the performance record, as well as some research on the industry outlook. Is new competition eating into established markets? Are new products threatening your company's position? Are rising wage costs putting excessive pressure on profit margins?

The Danger in Flat Earnings

In general, a flattening of earnings, unless it is accounted for by an obvious reason such as unusual expansion costs, portends bad news for investors. The flat earnings corporation is a rather insidious beast, and although many investors are loath to sell an often high-quality security because it is not vulnerable to substantial declines, the potential damage such a stock may accomplish must be examined.

In 1952, the range in price of the Frank G. Shattuck Co. (Schrafft's Restaurants) was 8⅛ to 10⅜. Assume that purchase of the stock was made at $9.00. This company afforded a good yield of almost 5 per cent at this price. Earnings for 1952 were 50¢ vs. 28¢ in the previous year.

From 1952 through 1957, the earnings for this company were as follows:

1952	1953	1954	1955	1956	1957
$.50	$.57	$.55	$.69	$.50	$.57

The price range of the stock during these years was:

1952	1953	1954	1955	1956	1957
8⅛–10⅜	7⅞–11⅛	8⅜–10¾	9⅝–11⅜	8⅛–11⅜	7¾–10⅝

The lackluster earnings performance of this company is reflected in the price of the stock during these years.

There was nothing wrong with an investor holding these shares during these five years if income was desired, but for the profit-minded investor F. G. Shattuck was a glaring disappointment.

During this five-year span, the Dow Jones Industrial Average went from slightly over 250 to a high of 525 in 1956, before settling to 440 during the 1957 market break. Thus, the averages more than doubled during this period while your stock did nothing.

It must be emphasized that we are not advocating sale of stock because it sits still for a period of time. This will happen to every stock during certain periods. What is to be concluded from this illustration is that flat, or narrow, earnings stocks afford poor prospects for profits. If you have purchased a stock which fails to perform well in earnings, it should be examined very closely, using the criteria of the Undervalued Method to determine if there is substantial evidence of *change* for the better. If there is no evidence of such improvement, the stock should be sold.

The Pressure of Earnings on Price

To complete the evidence of the impact of earnings on price, the Frank G. Shattuck Company proceeded from 1958 to earn as follows:

1958	1959	1960	1961	1962
$.70	$.93	$.95	$.80	—

Making allowances for the market madness which prevailed in late 1960 and 1961, the stock of this company ranged in price as follows:

1958	1959	1960	1961	1962
8⅝–16⅞	12⅜–19⅛	29⅛–12⅝	18⅞–31⅜	24–10

The pattern of prices in 1958 was a continuance of the previous five years ($8–$11), until in the final months the stock rose to over 16. In 1959, the stock stayed in this higher range and margins of profit increased from 3.2 per cent to 4 per cent. The earnings for the full year were 90 per cent higher than those realized just two years earlier.

In late 1960, the stock went up close to 30. At this price, it was selling over 30 times earnings.

In 1961, the stock started to slide back as the evidence accumulated that earnings were flattening out (the growth factor was missing). The stock completed its downward slide in 1962, as earnings declined to 80¢. At this writing the stock is selling at $13.00 per share.

When earnings are flat, the price will remain flat until evidence is presented by the corporation that strong earnings improvement will be made in the foreseeable future—one year.

The profit-minded investor is not interested in poor performance in price; he will therefore avoid the flat earnings stocks.

The result of lackluster corporate performance has been an attrition in price, inability to take advantage of attractive profit opportunities, and poor prospects for gains in the foreseeable future.

Flat earnings, or erratic earnings, in cyclical stocks are not promising avenues for continued investment.

THE CYCLICAL STOCK

The term "cyclical" is generally applied to those stocks whose earnings strength or weakness is dependent on the business cycle or fluctuations in the economy. Heavy-duty trucks, for example, are cyclical because surges in demand will depend on the construction industry and the general economic climate for business. Thus, in periods of economic plateaus or declines, the trucking industry (manufacturers) will have reduced sales and earnings, whereas in periods of prosperity truck sales will climb quickly to meet higher demands.

Generally, the term "cyclical" is used to indicate stocks or groups of stocks with relatively clear-cut and often rather short cycles of earnings. However, *most stocks are cyclical* in earnings, and therefore, in price.

Although it is true that we hear of many investors who bought a stock 20 years ago at $4.00 a share, and the stock is now selling at $80.00, we seldom hear repeated the story of the stock purchase at $80.00 that is now selling at $4.00. There is a reason for selling a stock, and the reason is that companies are like people. They do not normally get through life without running into some adversity. Adversity is what causes prices to drop, and, with a very few exceptions, there are few industries that we can safely categorize as immune from attrition.

For this reason—i.e., because no industrial stock is immune to changes in earnings, and therefore price—it is eminently reasonable to assume that all stocks will have ups and downs in earnings. Some companies will continue to grow in earnings for long periods of time, while others will do so for relatively short spans. The watchword for profits is to sell when the earnings improvement starts to decline.

Put Them Away, but DON'T Forget Them

As an example of the results of sitting with a stock, consider the case of Howe Sound Company. Assume purchase was made in 1953, at the mid-point of its price range for that year, or for a price of $15.00 per share. In 1953, it ranged from 21¼ to 9⅝. In 1954, the stock reached 20⅝, and each of the two succeeding years it sold higher than $26.00 per share (but never higher than 27¾). In 1957, it came down to a low of 5½, then in 1958 proceeded up to 14⅝. In 1959, the stock finished the year near its high of 27. In 1960, the stock was selling at over 24, before dropping off to below 14 per share. In 1961 and 1962, the stock declined from a high of 23¼ to slightly below $10.00. In early 1963, the stock was selling near $13.00 per share.

What was the result of holding Howe Sound for 10 years? Aside from dividends, none paid since 1957, the investor accomplished very little toward building his capital. We have only shown one stock but the example could be multiplied by hundreds. Oil stocks, auto stocks, chemicals, steels, coppers, aluminums, papers, aircrafts—all of them have in the past provided sound evidence of erratic earnings, and, therefore, sound reasons to effect sales. Business operates in the real world where everything does not go smoothly all the time. Utopia exists only in the minds of welfare state dreamers. In the real world, fire, flood, competition, strikes, Government action, human error, and myriad other possible catastrophes can become realities. Your job is simple: take advantage of the strong earnings and price movements, sell for a profit occasionally, and it will do you a tremendous lot of good.

Positive Aspects of the Cyclical Stock

Before leaving the subject of the cyclical stock, it is important to emphasize one point: *the cyclical stock is uniquely suited to the Undervalued Method of Selection and Investigation.*

It is often the case that a financially sound corporation, affording all of the inherent advantages of intrinsic value, will suffer declines in earnings during a weak "cycle." This type of corporation has the capability and potential of making a strong recovery in earnings. Using the "signal" to direct your attention to the stock and the follow-through of the investigation method provides a very strong weapon for discovering the changed direction of the depressed issue.

THE DECLINING EARNINGS CORPORATION

The stock that shouts out loud to be sold, and whose earnings are ignored, is an invitation to losses—deeper losses.

Selling out a stock whose earnings are declining is essential for the successful investor. No one is perfect, and neither will our judgement of facts be perfect. At some time, everyone has owned a stock that has defied analysis and done just the opposite of what is projected. This cannot be avoided, but what can be avoided is riding the stock into oblivion.

The most clear-cut sell situations are those with declining earnings. The situation which is crystal clear, indicating as a signal that earnings are down, would tell us immediately to investigate the stock.

Use the "third look" to run down the most recent year's, or period's, performance against the preceding period report. Just as we looked for a *change* upward in the earnings trend of a stock we contemplated buying, if we find a *change* downward in the earnings trend, the stock has provided us with a definite signal to sell.

The change in earnings that has occurred, or will occur, as a result of declining sales and higher costs, represents an immediate threat to the price of the stock.

The examples of price drops caused by earnings declines are very likely resting stubbornly in some of your portfolios right now. It is investment madness to retain them, when all indications are that the declines will become aggravated.

Hitting the Skids

American Bakeries is a well-established, high-dividend paying ($1.80 per share) stock with a fine financial structure. There is no long-term debt. There are only 1,766,000 shares outstanding, with $16,000,000 in cash and equivalent, and a current ratio of almost four-to-one (25.2 M current assets vs. 6.9 million current liabilities). The company has paid some dividend since 1928 without interruption, and on the basis of underlying strength the stock looks attractive.

Yet the earnings record looks like a ski-slope as seen from the top:

1957	1958	1959	1960	1961	1962
$3.49	$3.06	$3.02	$2.53	$2.18	$1.02

In 1957, the stock was $50.00 a share; in early 1963, the stock was $22.00. How about the position of the long-term investor who bought this stock in 1957 or 1958 or any other year? The range in price in 1961 was 36 to 47⅜, so it is apparent that the stock did not just skid down in price. There were opportunities to sell without grievous damage being inflicted. The point to be made is that declines can continue over a long period of time—often we do not know how long—yet all we can do is make decisions on the basis of facts available *now*, and project ahead our earnings estimates based on those facts. In the light of these facts, we make decisions. It should also be noted that, in the case of American Bakeries, a great deal of the price support achieved by the stock was a result of its $2.40 dividend. In 1961, the dividend was not covered by the $2.18 earnings, nor was it covered in 1962, and the dividend was reduced to $1.80.

Dividends will provide a degree of price protection until they are threatened by the failure of earnings to cover the dividend.

Why Did It Happen?

Why did American Bakeries (or the other baking stocks) suffer these declines? Was it management?

Although perhaps we can blame management for not getting out of the baking business, that would be somewhat extreme. The baking industry, and especially the large commercial bakers, were and are caught in the classic web of the welfare state, coupled with a classic case of old-fashioned capitalistic competition. The Government price-support structure on wheat (flour) forces higher product prices on consumers, which fact, coupled with normal wage and other material cost increases, has raised costs to a high level. The other side of the pincer consists of increased competition from chain stores' private labeling of bread and bakery products. This competition precludes price increases and in fact induces price cuts. The situation is further aggravated by the need for higher outlays for advertising to maintain established markets and to bite into the new competition. Thus management is, or can be, absolved of most of the blame for the poor performance. Although equipped and doubtless willing to take on new competition, it is very difficult to compete with the Government.

(It is not beyond the realm of probability that American Bakeries and other baking stocks will become attractive Undervalued candidates one day.)

Use the Fundamentals for Selling

The illustration of American Bakeries as a sell candidate at almost any time during the last six years is not an isolated case. There are hundreds of companies that have suffered from earnings declines, profit squeezes, adversity of some kind or another, which have consequently gone down in price. Many of these have been clear-cut cases that offered ample time and opportunity for investors to sell.

If a stock you own has earnings that have improved over the previous period reported, do not just accept the earnings as evidence that all is well. The indications of future trouble are often apparent months before the actual effect shown up in decreased earnings.

The elements that make up earnings—i.e., revenues and costs—will show cracks before earnings. This basis of evaluation will provide the impetus to sell, especially when the price of the stock is high in relation to earnings.

The fundamental facts of performance are the single lifeline available to investors. The "market" action, the whim of emotion, new product news, rumors, tips, and hopes, all create great dust storms that can obscure and becloud our own reasoning. It is very easy to become entranced with hopes as the market averages move up. At these times, it is all too easy to delude yourself that your "weaklings" will join the crowd. They probably will, for a short sprint, and that is the time to move out of them. Concentrate on your stocks, not on the market. Sell out if the indicators of performance dictate it.

If the basic precept of utilizing the corporation's performance can be applied as a beacon to guide us in our stock decisions, a great deal of grief and losses can be replaced with joy and profits.

You have now read about the Undervalued Method for buying stocks and have been exposed to the reasoning that underlies it. It is incumbent on the successful investor to utilize this method in his selling decisions.

THE FUNDAMENTALS AT WORK

For example, First National Stores earned $4.91 in 1956, slightly less than the $4.93 earned the previous year. The stock declined in 1956 from $61.00 to $47.00—once again, the effect of flat earnings. Assume that you discovered, in 1957, that sales were increasing and that margins of profit appeared to be improving. You purchased the stock during 1957 at its midrange of $52.00 (range 47–57). At the end of the year, the stock was selling at $57.00 and the following year (1958) saw the stock rise to $88.00, as investors crowded aboard because the 1957 earnings were up to $5.37 per share. Your original estimate that sales and margins of profit were improved was borne out as profit margins went from 3.3 per cent to 3.7 per cent, and sales increased to 531.5 M from 521.5 M.

During 1958, you witnessed a substantial rise in price of the stock. If you were as diligent in selling as in buying, you would have maintained your interest in the company's performance. In 1958, sales continued to climb, but margins of profit declined to 3.3 per cent. This should have triggered sufficient pressure to move you to take profits in the stock—*not* that the stock would not go higher, *not* because you were afraid of an overnight decline, *not* because the company could not fool you and show substantial improvement the following year, *but because* there was a sound reason provided, which indicated that earnings would be affected adversely by a decline in profit margin.

Go one step further and assume that you decided to wait out the year, and see what final results were achieved by the company. This is not a bad course of action, and in the case of First National, the full-year results showed earnings of $5.02, down from the $5.28 earned in 1957. The sales were up and the margin of profit was down. This decline in earnings should have been the final spur needed to sell. Many investors did sell, and succeeded in dropping the stock to a low of $71.00 near the end of the year.

It is a constant source of frustration to buy a stock at a reasonable price and watch it rise in price as the stock responds to its earnings development, and then to watch the profits wither away as sell signals are ignored.

There are unquestionably many stocks whose performance data is so nebulous that a clear-cut decision cannot be made. There are stocks in the gray area, whose earnings projections are just too cloudy for definition. As a general rule, when in serious doubts as to the earnings direction of the corporation, sell out the stock. There are entirely too many unknowns in even the best of stocks to afford us the luxury of adding an all-important unknown to our scale of risk.

Using the Second Look in Selling

In the second look of the Undervalued Method, five of the six steps are concerned with the operating statement of the corporation. By measuring your stocks against this yardstick—sales; cost of goods sold; gross profit; cost of sales; net profit—you will have an effective, quick measure of the *current* performance characteristics of your company for each period's financial report.

If sales are flattening or declining, or if margins of profit are falling down, you have been provided with a valid reason to investigate further, with the objective of protecting your profits and guarding against losses. We say "investigate further" to protect you from selling *if* the declines noted can be attributed to a temporary, nonrecurring situation that may have affected sales or margin during the period reported.

Although sales and margins of profit are not the only two factors that can affect earnings, they are the most sensitive antenna available for indications of weakness or potential weakness.

Operating Indicators and the First Look

It must be emphasized here that the survey of the company, brief as it is, using the second look should be combined with the first three steps of the first look, namely: price; earnings; price earnings ratio.

If any tell-tale weakness appears in the performance section of a growth, or high price to earnings stock, it should have the same effect on you as a red flag to a bull. Charge for the telephone and sell! The reason for this is contained in the very nature of the growth stock. Investors have bid the stock to high levels in *anticipation* of a future, continued high percentage of growth in earnings. If any clouds appear that threaten to dampen or defer the growth in earnings, disappointed investors will have a tendency to stampede out of the stock.

In all cases, earnings declines are a positive threat to prices. In high price earnings stocks, the threat is devastating.

As was mentioned in an earlier section, dividends tend to provide a floor for stock prices when the yield starts to approach the current corporate bond yields. However, dividends are not guaranteed; they must be paid from earnings. When earnings fail to cover dividends, it is a foolhardy board of directors that will permit the situation to last very long. If earnings cannot be increased, they will fulfill their obligation to your company by cutting the dividend. The dividend cut will normally provide good reason for further declines in price.

Because we attempt to anticipate declines in earnings just as we attempt to anticipate improvements in earnings, we cannot and do not prescribe closing our eyes to facts.

If you have not been able to forecast earnings weakness and it occurs, do not sit still for very long. Determine why it occurred, and if there is little reason to predict an early return to strong earnings, sell the stock.

Keep constantly in mind that the changes in earnings, either up or down, are the final arbiters of the direction of price. Do not be stoic about your losers and tell yourself how tough you are and that "you can take it like a man" while sitting with them. All of us can take losses because usually we do not have an option, but the profit-minded investor sells the weak stock to buy a strong stock and improve his opportunities to recover his losses.

SELLING ON PRICE

When vulnerability to decline balances or outweighs probable gains, the prudent investor will sell.

In 1961, McGraw-Hill Publishing Company ranged in price from 43 to 30¾ on earnings for the year 1960 of $1.16 per share. In 1961, the company earned $1.03. Since 1957, the company had proceeded in about the same earnings range.

During 1962, the price dropped on the stock, as did the rest of the stock market. In the spring of 1963, the stock was selling at or near $23.00 per share.

Harking back to 1961 when the stock was selling at $35.00, the investor would be holding a stock selling at a multiple of 30 times earnings (1960 earnings). At that time, the Dow Jones averages were selling at about 23 times earnings. McGraw-Hill was richly priced for such a staid earnings performance. The stockholder was holding the stock for further gains, but his risks of decline were greater than his potential gains.

Realizing that publishing stocks were "in" that year, we must still maintain a sense of proportion in our investments. Does it seem fair to assume that investors will go berserk and drive a sluggish earnings corporation to 60 times earnings? Even 40 times requires a great deal of imagination. It must then be apparent that the investor keep awake to changes in price that carry stocks too far ahead of their earnings potential. When this overenthusiasm occurs, it can only be sustained by the corporation producing earnings improvements consonant with the price. In this area, most stocks fail to deliver on their promise.

The High Price-Earning Stock

The only stocks that have or deserve to have extraordinary price earnings multiples are those that are producing extraordinary earnings growth, and that indicate that there is every likelihood that this growth will continue for an indefinite period in the future.

Every year, investors thrust new candidates forward to don the mantle of consistent and sensational growth in earnings. Whole industries, or groups of stocks, are accorded this accolade of high price earnings ratios, *yet most* of them *fail* to deliver.

Do not be afraid to cut and run when prices start reaching the stratosphere. You will possibly miss some further profits, but the chances are excellent you will protect actual profits.

The area of selling based on price alone is an extremely nebulous one, in that each situation will vary from the next in terms of earnings, price earnings level, and so on. But there are not any sanctified areas of the market. The healthiest blue chip, sturdiest utility, or wildest risk stock are all subject at some point in time to overenthusiastic buying. The basic premise to keep in mind is that glamourous investing, like glamourous living, can bring on a hangover.

The element of greed, coarse as the word may sound, is often the cause of holding on too long to a particular stock.

JUDGMENT IN SELLING

It is to be hoped that the fundamentals will provide an effective tool to warn you of the threat of decline, but sometimes fundamentals are no help at all in the overpriced stock. When *your* stock is selling at $25.00 per share on earnings of 60¢ per share, it is most difficult to find any reason for selling *except* that you may cold-bloodedly calculate that, if it dropped to 15 times earnings, it would be selling at $9.00 per share. At this time, you must weigh the chances for the stock moving up to $30.00 (or 50 times earnings) against the possibility of decline to very much lower levels. Your only defense against "hoping" it will go to 30 times, or 40 times, ad infinitum, is to realize that your fellow investors are not lacking intelligence. If you cannot find a substantial reason to establish that future earnings (not five years from now) will justify the current price, you will be better off in a better quality earnings stock selling at a reasonable level of price to earnings.

It is *not possible* for anyone to define what a "reasonable" price earnings ratio is or should be for any stock. However, it is possible to put reason and judgment into investment decisions. It is also not possible nor intended that a comprehensive review of the many facets of varying price earnings influences be covered here. What is intended is to provide a framework of reference for making selling decisions in stocks that have appreciated very rapidly and to very high prices in relation to earnings.

Perspective on Growth

New companies or small companies with low capitalization and relatively small markets for their products can show great growth in earnings on a percentage basis if their product or service comes into new-found demand. Because they are starting from a lower *base*, their growth factor can be substantial. For instance, General Time Corporation increased its earnings from 29¢ in 1958 to 91¢ in 1959. Sales (or revenues) went from 47.6 M to 59.2 M for an increase of almost 25 per cent. The margin of profit (operating profit) increased on the higher sales to 5.6 per cent from 1.3 per cent, and the price of the stock went to 33⅛, or slightly more than 36 times earnings in mid-1960.

General Foods Corporation, in the same period, increased its sales by $34,000,000 (vs. $12,000,000 for General Time), for a percentage increase of slightly more than 3 per cent. The margin of profit also improved, and the stock price in 1960 went to 75½ on earnings of 2.48 for the full year of 1959.

The point to be made is that a relatively small dollar increase on the small company can have an enormous effect on earnings, *but*, because the company is small, the converse of this case is also true: a relatively small decrease can have a devastating effect on earnings. The high price of the stock responding to the growth in earnings provides no cushion of time for selling decisions. The stumble in performance can send prices plummeting. Thus, General Time in 1960 increased sales by one million, or slightly more than 2 per cent, but earnings disappeared to a deficit of 36¢. In a period of five months, the price dropped to a low of 12½ from the high of 33.

This is not an exercise in dissuading from investment in small growth companies. Every major corporation started out that way, but we are attempting to display the risks that are inherent in the fast-moving stocks. Although price alone is a rather weak basis for sale of a stock, it must suffice, because the investor often has no other yardstick.

Safeguard Against Emotion

Emotion is a basis for many *groups* of stocks being bid up to overenthusiastic levels. When the market has elected an industry or group to wear the laurel of "glamour," all reason seems to desert investors. The chosen group is wafted high on a crest of enthusiastic enchantment. It is always our fondest hope to participate in such waves, but also to keep our feet on the ground while the swell is building up. The important fact to keep in mind is that emotion spends itself and, further, that it usually goes to extremes. If you are fortunate enough and astute enough to have stocks in the currently favored group, keep your balance and be prepared to sell as the price earnings ratio starts to mount. We cannot fix a target level for a universal price earnings "norm," but we can apply common sense to prices. If the industry's average rate of growth is 7 per cent per year, and price ratios start to reach a point where 5 to 10 years' compounded growth are needed to make the prices reasonable in the "normal market," do not be afraid to take profits and miss the highs. Emotion usually carries the seeds of its own decline.

The *general* rule for growth is that it does not come without interruptions, even if the trend continues upward. If signs or hints of an interruption appear, not only in the growth but also in the rate of growth, then relinquish your hold on the stocks. There are, of course, exceptions to this rule, and the present favorite of all growth stocks, I.B.M., is an outstanding example. But from 1946 to 1953, even the "greatest" had an erratic growth record. It had, however, the proven growth rate of approximately 20 per cent a year, coupled with an anticipation of continuance of this rate of growth, which accords this stock its great favor. These facts, coupled with the truly dynamic growth in demand of its unique products and services, comprise the bulwark of investors' faith and judgement.

The I.B.M.'s are rare exceptions, and most companies do not reach this stature. So keep emotion down and be willing and eager to take advantage of market favorites on their way up.

There could be, and perhaps one day there will be, a complete book on selling stocks that elaborates all of the possible ramifications entering into such a decision. For most purposes, however, it is more than sufficient to predicate your decisions on the corporate performance. For the second major selling reason, you must defend yourself from greed with reasoned judgment, not on what you hope will be, but on what probably will be in the light of past performance.

Do not be afraid to sell when prices are high; that is why you bought the stock in the first place.

SELLING (OR NOT SELLING) FOR TAXES

It would not be possible to write about selling stocks without at least brushing up against the tax selling problem.

The effects of the capital gains tax are more far-reaching on prices than most of us realize. The long-term income investor who bought Otis Elevator at a price of $9.00 per share in 1952 entertains a great reluctance to sell this stock at $60.00 per share. This investor would be faced with a maximum tax of $1300 on his $6000 sale of 100 shares. The result of his reluctance is to withhold effectively from the market his shares of Otis Elevator. We can multiply this investor by thousands, and these shares by millions, to see that, over a long period of time, this cutback in available shares will result in fiercer competition for available stock. This competition will result, and has resulted, in often artificially high prices.

The impact of taxes is very great. It often looms too large in the considerations of many investors, causing them to suffer price declines that could reasonably have been avoided.

If you are in the stock market to achieve profits, then taxes are a purely secondary consideration. When they interfere with actions that should be taken, they are causing you more than the expense of tax payments.

To be realistic about taxes, it is well to remember that about the only contribution most of us make to the preservation of the free enterprise system is through our taxes. We should pay with a prayer of thanks for the hard-won right to invest what and when we like in profit-oriented ventures. Many of us feel the capital gains tax is inequitable and serves as a stern anchor on venture capital, but in spite of the drag, we can live with it and make money.

Tax considerations are not to be treated disdainfully. Remember that capital gains rates are usually lower than ordinary income. Keep taxes in their proper perspective.

ON INVESTING

Investing requires courage. The most amazing element in the free enterprise system is the dauntless "guts" of the hard-working wage-earner putting his hard-earned dollars on the line to back his convictions. All of the grief and problems that can arise in any company are scorned by the faith of the individual that "his" company will perform well. It is a mark of the greatness of this society that a blind newsdealer, a high school teacher, a Connecticut police sergeant, an ad agency art director, a merchant seaman—all find a common ground comprised of vision, faith, and confidence in investing for *their own profit*, and thereby creating the venture capital needed for the profit of the nation.

Wall Street has been scarred by the abuses inflicted by the few, but its strength is apparent in the demonstrated ability to grow and serve the capital needs of the nation, and indeed the world, because of the courage of some 17,000,000 American investors.

Courage is needed, but knowledge is indispensable. Knowledge of what your corporations are doing is the single greatest defense against losses and the strongest weapon available for extracting profit.

Do not let emotion get in the way of facts. Play to win and you will.

14

Sidelights and Summary

Some sidelights on investing in general and a summary of investing in the Undervalueds.

A REVIEW OF THE UNDERVALUED METHOD

The Undervalued Method is predicated on the *fact* that stock *prices* will *follow* the anticipated or *actual earnings* trend of the corporation. The power of earnings lies in the fact that they provide the incentive for investors to buy and sell stocks. Therefore, earnings and anticipation of them cause prices to change.

This book outlines a valid method of investigating the financial and performance characteristics of a corporation. The investigation is designed to provide not just information about what has happened, but an interpretation of that information designed to tell you what *will probably happen*.

The basis for forecasting earnings lies in the fact that overnight changes in direction are the exceptions, not the rule. The fact is that corporations are like the boxers who telegraph their punches.

When a company shows strong earnings improvement, it is ridiculous to believe that such improvement was the result of luck or that it occurred very quickly. Improvement or decline result from decisions made months or perhaps years before the fact of earnings change shows up.

The decisions relative to expanding a sales force or building a new plant are remote from the fact of current earnings, but the *pattern of change* is more often than not revealed in the operating statements.

The earnings indicators, the first five steps of the second look, represent the clearest picture of the operating trend of the corporation.

It is not only earnings, but the trend in earnings, which will combine to provide you with profits.

The "Theory of Momentum" is the cornerstone of the validity of making projections. The company which is showing higher sales, improved margins of profit, lower costs, and improved earnings, in the first quarter (or third or fourth) will *very likely* continue to show such improvements in succeeding periods. The price of the stock should continue to respond to the upward pressure in earnings.

The trend in performance is what makes possible reasonable earnings projections. The flattening or declines in earnings are, likewise, a benefit in utilizing the earnings indicators for selling signals.

THE APPLICATION OF THE UNDERVALUED METHOD

Although the purpose of investing is profit, the effort needed to achieve that goal lies in the investigation preceding investments. Because profits come from stocks and not from the "market," this book was directed toward using information from and about individual stocks to lead you into profit-oriented situations.

The details of each step throughout the investigation may result in an impression that considerable effort is needed for each investigation; this is not true.

The "signal" is one you have been reading about and noting during your daily reading of the newspapers.

The direction provided by the signal to look at the stock is equally painless.

The design of the Undervalued Method is to achieve the greatest results from the least possible effort.

When a directional signal is noted, the first look provides an easy answer as to whether or not you should look further.

When, on the basis of the first look, a stock shows sufficient promise, you begin to put some time and effort into the investigation.

The second look provides a strong indication of where the subject corporation is headed. The so-called "earnings indicators" provide the strongest spur to further investigation, or a stiff, straight arm to stop you in your tracks.

It is apparent that the third look will only be called into play in those situations that have been screened for assets, earnings, price, and direction of earnings. Depending on the diligence of the investor, the number of times this "work step" will be needed will be very few in comparison to the total number of stocks looked at.

With practice, the first look takes a matter of minutes—a scanning of pertinent facts. The second look becomes only slightly more burdensome, and the burden rests to some extent on the availability of one of the financial reference works. The third look deserves some effort because it is the final stage preceding investment of your *money*.

GETTING RESULTS

There is a tremendous opportunity for substantial profits in common stocks. The opportunities are available to all—not "insiders," not institutions, not "they"; they are there for *you*.

The institutions and the professionals use investigation, research, and analysis to improve their opportunities for gains. There is no reason why you cannot do the same thing.

The Undervalued Method will not make you an analyst, but it will make you a realistic investor capable of weighing facts, making judgments of probabilities, and improving your chances for gains.

There is a fascination about knowledge of stocks that exists in few other areas of endeavor.

The prospect of having money work for you in such an obvious and easily followed market is in itself a thrilling opportunity. To effect purchase of a stock and watch it respond to the impact of earnings you had projected is a double-barrelled satisfaction: first, because you have made money; second, and perhaps more important, because you have seen at work the fact of stock prices following earnings. This development of confidence in a valid basis of reasoning will enable you to develop a philosophy of investment.

AN INVESTMENT PHILOSOPHY

Planning is a part of every facet of our lives, and it is especially essential to successful investing. Because of the marvelous diversity of tastes, interests, and aims of the human race, no one can dictate what your philosophy of investment should be. But because of the nature of equity investments, we can elaborate somewhat on the necessity of planning for the profit-minded investor (as distinguished from the income or defensive investor).

The most obvious requirement in investing is to use only funds that are above and beyond your individual and family needs.

The fact must be accepted that money is a tool used to make more money through the medium of common stocks. This concept will enable you to eliminate the emotion of "falling in love with" stock, and determining to "stick with it through thick and thin," regardless of the consequences.

Determine before you start investing what your objectives are—not just profits; everyone wants those. For example, a very small investor who earns a substantial salary and has sizable participation in an excellent pension program had a portfolio of eight stocks, of fairly good quality, amounting to $1600 in value. He believed in diversification. His aim was to make money, but his method was self-defeating. Capable and willing to take risks, he was taking eight paths when he could only afford one, or at the most, two. With eight stocks, such as five shares of Montgomery Ward (cost $33.00 per share), ten Ryder Systems (cost $24.00 per share), and so on, it will be evident that substantial increases in value were needed in *all* stocks for this investor to make any appreciable gains.

By selling the eight stocks and then reinvesting the $1600 in *two* stocks both selling under $20.00 per share, this investor, by dint of the Undervalued Method, accomplishes two things. (1) He purchased stocks of reasonably good quality, offering the best possible protection of his capital, i.e., earnings. (2) He concentrated his risks in two stocks of reasonably low price, affording him the chance to buy a sufficient number of shares so that, if his projections and investigation are correct, when the stocks go up in value he will realize substantial gains.

This investor could afford risks but was taking risks that were unsuitable to his goals. He needed a change in his method of investing to accomplish his ends.

Some investors who can ill afford high risks are invested in wild speculations affording minimal protection. Others are in solid-income stocks on a margin account, whereby the income is devoured by margin interest charges. Not all methods are suitable to any particular investor, but overdiversification can be as self-defeating as overconcentration. Estimate where you want to go and determine for yourself the most effective way of getting there.

Buy the corporation, not the stock, and sell the same way. Do not think in terms of the stock's performance. Be realistic and think in terms of the corporate earnings performance. This will greatly ease buying and selling decisions.

Do not be afraid to take profits. When your stock reaches a price level that is fully or nearly in line with similar stocks in the same industry, and when it is evident that further gains will require extraordinary buying enthusiasm, do not be afraid to sell. This is especially true when the fundamentals reflect a flattening of earnings.

Be prepared to take an occasional loss. Losses happen to everyone. Think in terms of money. If your dollars are tied up in a stock that has failed to perform and there is evidence that such failure may be prolonged, sell and get into a stronger stock, where your money may work better for you.

Investigate before you invest.

COMMENTS ON THE TECHNICAL ASPECTS OF STOCK TIMING

The "chartist" or technician can provide a substantial degree of assistance in the timing of purchases and sales.

The developing patterns of investor interest, as revealed by price and volume movements of a stock, can be of great assistance in targeting buy and sell points in particular issues.

The chart interpretations can be surprisingly accurate and have understandably attracted a substantial following among investors. But charts are surface manifestations of the fundamentals of corporate performance.

A realistic approach to the fundamentals should be a must for even the purest chartist. The reason is that direction of earnings can provide the trend line of price direction. The imposition of technical, or market, pressures atop the fundamentals can therefore provide a further refinement in buying and selling.

The Signal

Perhaps one of the areas most liable to confusion in the Undervalued Method is the "signal." The presentation made in the stocks illustrated may lend the *false* impression that almost any signal heralds a change that will be reflected in the price of the stock in a short period of time. This is far from true.

The signals are the best, most efficient, and most rewarding method of leading you into promising investment situations, but they require some effort. Many an investigation will curl up and die on the first look. It is strongly recommended that stocks with promise be noted and reviewed as their quarterly reports appear. This type of activity can bear rich rewards.

If a situation is located but it is not yet ripe, do not forget it—watch it!

NEGATIVE ATTITUDES TOWARD INVESTING

In most instances, it is the height of folly to set target prices for stocks. The investor who owns a $15.00 stock and exclaims noisily that "it's going to $100" is hurting his chances for profit. Assume the stock goes to $30 and mental repetition of this target of $100 has brought sweet, pink visions of sudden affluence to this investor, preventing him from viewing the performance of the corporation and the stock in a realistic fashion. When you invest in common stocks, be prepared for anything. Do not close your mind as you would close a book when you finish it. Remember that your work is just starting when you buy. It may be that years will pass and that the corporate performance will leave little to be desired. If so, you will continue with the stock, but if earnings start to decline, take your winnings and leave.

When a stock is purchased, based on a given set of facts that indicate that improvement in performance is soon to be realized, you will purchase with confidence. However, if one week or one month later these facts have changed, have the courage to face reality and sell.

Undervalued Stocks crop up everywhere, with every shade and degree of potential. Many investors carry bias and prejudice into their investment decisions. The all too frequent, "I do not invest in rails," is about as sensible as the bustle. Maybe you do not like the rails but you do like profits. If there is a good profit potential in a railroad stock, leave your mind wide enough open to investigate. Many investors did not like defense issues, or discount stores, or any one of a number of industries that later proved to be highly profitable. It does not make sense to condemn all the companies in a given industry if that industry is depressed. However—and that is a big "however"—it is generally true that individual industry depression will, as a rule, tend to keep all stocks in that industry depressed. The point to be remembered is—do not close your mind. Changes do occur and time passes quickly. Be prepared to look critically at any situation at any time. Test it, evaluate it, judge it. If all is well, buy it and then keep watching it.

HANDLING THE INACTIVE STOCK

Suppose for a moment that the stock you hold is in the gray never-never land of consistent inactivity. Suppose that years pass and your stock lies there flagrant with ennui. Fear of selling the stock is heightened by the possibility that as soon as you do, it will skyrocket in price. Yet the nagging feeling persists that, when five years have passed, the stock will have continued its lethargic performance. What do you do?

Because this is a "gray" area covering a host of possibilities, re-examine the company's income statement and balance sheet as you would in the third look of the examination. Use the most recent reports to bring the performance record up to date.

CONCLUSION

The junket through the vale of the Undervalueds is completed. The rather limited segment of the market where Undervalueds are found is broadened tremendously by the scope of the principles of the fundamentals of a stock.

The most significant element of this brief presentation is the relationship of stock prices to corporate earnings. Elemental as this appears to be, it should be evident that application of this principle should result in profits.

The ability to make fair projections of earnings based on interim reports, past performance, coupled with the cross-checks of margin of costs and profits, is a strong guide pointing you toward a more accurate evaluation of potential worth.

The expedient of using historic price patterns to determine relative price position of the stock, at the time of the investigation, is designed to provide further protection in the area of timing the purchase. The fact that marginal companies may at times be under consideration makes this an important consideration.

If you are faced with an investment decision in a stock that is evidencing very strong earnings, and which has already appreciated somewhat in value, do not disqualify this stock from consideration because you missed the "low." This admonition is directed at sound, quality stocks where fear of buying at the "high" might prevent you from realizing substantial future gains. A Singer Manufacturing, for example, will not require the same harsh demands as a Standard Fruit. Be arbitrary—absolutely arbitrary—in your demands on the Undervalued that is emerging from losses, but do not anticipate buying well-rated stocks below historic value levels.

The area of the balance sheet is undoubtedly the most colorless section of the investigation. It is difficult to get excited over "an increase of 8 per cent in net current asset value," or the "elimination of a portion of long-term debt," yet this section cannot be overlooked. Assets and liabilities affect earnings and growth; hence they affect the profit-and-loss potential of your stock. One day, in some stock, an examination of liabilities may show a sharp increase in short-term bank loans, which may in turn create sufficient doubts to save you from possible losses in the stock. (Please understand that bank loans are not *always* an adverse sign. Bankers are somewhat notorious for their unwillingness to loan money out of a sense of good fellowship, so that repayment ability looms large in these warm-hearted gestures.)

The operating section of the Undervalued Method is at once more exciting and more meaningful because it provides the all-important "direction of movement." Your direction will be straighter through investigation before investing.

The Undervalued Method appears to be extensive, but it is in reality quite brief. Some factors have been completely ignored in an attempt to provide the greatest safety with the least work. The marriage of expedience and thoroughness is at best uneasy, yet the value of an investigation of this type cannot help but be rewarding.

The stock market is not static. Changes in the corporation result in changes in the price of the stock. Discerning those changes should prove to be an avenue of profit. The Undervalueds exist along that avenue.

Appendix

Cash flow = Net Income after Taxes
+ Depreciation Charges
+ Depletion Charges
+ Amortization Charges
+ Extraordinary Charges to Reserve

Since the corporate tax structure has become so complex, involving as it does depreciation, depletion, and amortization as deductions from net income before taxes, it has been increasingly difficult for investors to get an unclouded view of just how much cash is being generated by the corporation.

Cash flow provides the answer to that problem. By taking net income after taxes and adding back the amounts charged to depreciation, the amount charged for depletion (in companies that are engaged in mining, oil, etc.) and amortization, nonrecurring charges to reserves, the cash flow of the corporation is derived. These items of depreciation, which can be a sizable amount of money, depletion, and amortization, are bookkeeping deductions from income. The dollars are not paid out, and thus cash flow provides a yardstick used by many analysts to provide an indication of the ability of the company to finance its expansion, provide dividends, or provide money for acquisitions. The flow of cash can have a strong influence on the future course of a corporation, because a high cash flow provides substantial flexibility to management. Cash flow, however, is an extremely nebulous influence on stock prices. Its determination opens the door to a great number of analytical problems. The accounting methods for treating depreciation, such as the declining-balance method, the straight-line method, the sum-of-the-digits method, can all produce greatly varied results, and add to the specialized knowledge needed to interpret the possible impact on the corporation.

Cash flow can serve as an excellent indicator of corporate strength, but for the Undervalued Method, the end-results of earnings margins, assets, and so on, are strong pillars on which to rest.

Floating supply of stock. The term "floating supply" refers to the free or available stock of a corporation as opposed to the amount that is closely held by institutions or family groups related to the founders of the corporation.

If a corporation has 1,000,000 shares of stock outstanding, but 800,000 of these shares are held by the family of the founder of the corporation, the floating supply of the stock would only be 200,000 shares.

The floating supply is an important consideration when buying or selling the stock because in "thin" markets (few shares available) the price changes can be quite sharp in response to very light buying and selling pressures.

The growth in size of institutional investors such as trusts, insurance companies, foundations, and mutual funds further diminishes the amount of stock available as these groups gobble up great chunks of stock. Such holders cannot be considered to restrict the floating supply in the pure sense of the term, because they will and do sell their holdings in response to corporate performance.

The floating supply of a stock can and does have a substantial impact on the price performance of that stock, but for purposes of investigation it will not constitute a part of the investigation.

Inventories. One of the most difficult parts of the financial statement to analyze is that of inventories. The reason is that diversity of industries, multiplied by the diversity of items produced, further multiplied by the components of those products, results in a staggering variety of items. Add to this the variations in valuation of inventories and their dollars-and-cents impact on the balance sheet, and some recognition of the problem of analysis can be obtained.

Although it is a problem in evaluation, the greatest defense provided the investor is the basically conservative approach of most corporations in business practices, including realistic inventory evaluation. This factor, coupled with the forces of competition and the drive for profitable operation, predisposes the corporation to state, realistically, inventory valuations.

Inventories often comprise the great bulk of asset values for many concerns, so that though the variety of items may be bewildering, the common sense approach to inventory examination is invaluable. If a plumbing fixture manufacturer is carrying inventories that are almost equal to one year's sales, it does not take too much logic to decide that either inventories are overstated or that inventories are backed up too deeply in his warehouse and that sales are not meeting production.

The value of inventories in analyzing a stock can be inestimable, but with today's diversification into many areas of different industries by so many corporations, inventory analysis becomes more and more difficult.

Though it is not incorporated in the Undervalued Method of investigation because of the dangers of misinterpretation and misuse, the inventory approach to sales and earnings forecasting is briefly noted here with the *admonition that it is extremely dangerous, quite difficult to use in many cases, and impossible in others.*

Many corporations forecast their sales by building up or decreasing their inventories of raw and finished goods. The basis for this forecasting is the intimate knowledge of "the market" for its products by management and the ever-present necessity for management to anticipate demand so that it can fill orders. "Wrong" forecasts can be expensive in lost sales, and, more important, in lost markets. The investor can participate in these anticipations of managements forecasts by very closely watching inventory build-ups and declines.

If Company "A" normally turns over its inventory 12 times per year (this is quite a high turnover and is used only for purposes of illustration), and their normal year-end inventory is one-tenth of annual sales, it would be quite promising to see that, for the current year, inventories are shown at one-sixth of sales, or a 100 per cent increase. This is where such "fishing expeditions" really get treacherous, because the inventory build-up may be a result of lagging sales. If the sales for the final quarter of the year were up, and the finished and raw inventories are up, you *may* multiply the current year-end inventory by the "normal" inventory turnover (12) and obtain a projection of sales for the year. By taking the operating net profit rate for the final quarter shown, and applying it to the projected sales figures, you may come up with a projected earnings figure for the coming year. By relating estimated earnings to current price and current price earnings ratio, an *estimate* of value of the stock may be reached.

Although it sounds fairly reasonable to make such projections, it must be apparent that it is *extremely dangerous* because:

(1) There may be special considerations on the part of management for building inventories, which have nothing to do with increased sales projections. Fear of higher raw material prices in the future, for example, may have induced them to buy more than usual.

(2) Management, like stock brokers, can make an occasional mistake.

(3) Most important of all is the fact that inventory projections are more dangerous than ever because of the advent of computer systems, which enable management to maintain inventory controls which were undreamed of 10 years ago. The entire field of inventory valuation, as an indicator of sales and earnings, and therefore price, is in a complete state of flux.

(In spite of the above warning, such projection computations can be challenging and informative for those who are so inclined.)

The heavy emphasis on the risks involved in inventory forecasting is not intended to discourage investors completely from pursuing a slightly deeper investigation of the corporation under study. The more you know, the stronger you will be, and we anticipate you will be richer also.

Inventory forecasting requires work. Whereas a four-year review of the corporation is required in the Undervalued Method, a *ten-year* review of inventory patterns is needed before you can even determine if such a forecast is possible. The *only* corporations that could possibly qualify for such a forecast are those evincing a steady, discernible pattern of inventory-to-sales relationship. If the pattern or ratio is erratic, it is worthless to continue. If, however, you find that in 1953 inventories were down at the year-end and sales were down for the following year (1954), and if a turnover average of inventories follows a measurable pattern in relation to the following year's sales, and if the consistency of this pattern is strong, you will have good grounds for fitting your inventory projections alongside your other earnings projections (annualized current period earnings, rate of sales improvement, operating net margins, etc.) to serve as a reinforcement of your findings.

Do not put too much faith in inventory projections. However, it should be apparent that inventory investigation is a worthwhile pursuit of and by itself because it is one of the best "tale bearers" about management that exists. If you find that inventory turnover is improving, you will know that more efficient use of working capital is being made. The savings in cost of warehousing inventories, the savings in cost of interest by preventing dollars from lying idly in dead inventories—these and other benefits will find their way into the earnings column and will help to pay you with higher prices on your stock.

Inventories are vital and meaningful. A close look at them will be profitable.

Liquidity of assets. The existence of "strong" asset value in a corporation is not in itself a dollars-and-cents element of protection to the investor, because the "liquidity" or convertibility of those assets into cash is the final measure of the worth of the assets.

Asset or book value, as covered in the text, is a strong guide or indication of value, not an absolute value. The reason for this is that the corporation itself can only *estimate* the value of assets. As one financial analyst put it, "The only time you can determine the value of assets absolutely is when you sell them."

Corporations generally use conservative estimates of value of assets, but in some cases even conservative valuations result in overstatements of value. Thus a piece of equipment valued at $100,000 may become worthless if it becomes obsolete.

The other possibility is the understatement of asset values. If a company carries a piece of metropolitan real estate on its books at cost, and the real estate has been owned by the corporation for 40 years, the "liquidity value" of the property may be 40 times its "book" or stated value.

A corporation's assets should be examined not only from the viewpoint of amount of the assets, but also the *kind* of assets. If the assets consist of plants and equipment, the age of the plant could be such that the market or resale value is negligible because it is old or inefficient. Equipment such as machinery, once used and installed, can be a severe headache for the seller when he tries to find a buyer.

An inventory of heavy equipment for a capital goods manufacturer may be much less liquid than a consumer goods manufacturer's inventories.

Since inventories often comprise a large segment of the assets, consideration from a practical standpoint should therefore be shown for the type of industry that is being investigated.

Many conservative investors automatically recompute book or asset values to an estimated liquidity value by reducing the assets as much as fifty per cent, depending on the corporation and its industry type, to obtain a realistic valuation of what actual protection the assets should afford. This step is taken in cases where losses have been severe and a danger of forced liquidation exists.

Other income. Nonrecurring items. Fixed charges. It is evident from the steps of the third look that an often sizeable discrepancy exists between net profit (from operations) and net income after taxes for the corporation.

The discrepancy was not treated in the text to avoid adding extraneous items to the basic examination method.

There are any number of charges and extraordinary items which can and do affect net income. For our purposes, we shall treat three broad categories that serve as additions to or deductions from operating profit.

The XYZ Corporation—Income Statement

Net Sales	$100,000
Cost of Goods Sold	75,000
Gross Profit	25,000
Cost of Sales	4,000
Operating Profit	21,000
Interest Earned and Dividends Received	500 M
Other Income	400 M
Total Income	21,900 M
Interest Expense	300 M
Profit-Sharing Provision	800 M
Other Deductions	100 M
Net Income Before Fed. Taxes	20,700 M

Provision for Fed. and Foreign Taxes	11,385 M
State and Local Taxes	50 M
Net Income to Surplus	9,365 M

The simplified income statement shows an operating profit of 21M, with a net income of 9.3M.

The items that make up this difference vary greatly as to types and amounts.

Other income. Any income received by the corporation that originates from a source other than its operation is classified as other income. If a manufacturer of industrial belting realizes income from royalties on patents held by the corporation, these payments would be shown under other income or royalty income. The reason for such classification of income is to present a clear-cut picture of the operating company by not distorting the earning ability with outside elements.

Dividend income realized from securities owned by the corporation, or rents received from tenants occupying company-owned buildings, are similar examples.

Nonrecurring items. If a corporation sold a piece of real estate and realized a profit on the sale, such a profit would be classified as "nonrecurring capital gains." The classification "nonrecurring" informs you immediately that a special situation has created a profit opportunity for the corporation. This income cannot be anticipated to repeat itself.

The same case is true in the event of nonrecurring losses, such as a law-suit loss. Nonrecurring gains and losses cannot weigh too heavily in evaluation of a security unless the magnitude of the gain or loss is so great as to affect the operations of the corporation.

Fixed charges. Fixed charges can create some problems in that they can be confused with fixed expenses. Fixed operating expenses relate to plant rental. Fixed charges, on the other hand, constitute a deduction from net income and are comprised of items such as interest charges on long-term debt and amortization of that debt. These charges are fixed by the term of the loan agreement, or indenture in the case of a bond. Such charges must be paid whether or not they are earned. The provision of a reserve, or sinking fund, for repayment of the principal of the loan may also constitute a fixed charge.

Return on invested capital. Grading management on its efficiency has been confined in the Undervalued Method to operating ratios and the final arbiter of efficiency: earnings.

There is another valuable tool used by many investors and analysts in evaluating corporate efficiency: return on invested capital.

By dividing total capitalization (amount invested in the corporation) into total net operating profit (net profit before taxes), we obtain the percentage of total capital which is being produced by the invested dollars.

This test is used to determine whether the corporation is using its investment profitably. There are, however, several ramifications involved in the use of the ratio of return on invested capital, not the least of which are the variations possible in the base figures used (net worth in lieu of invested capital, for example).

Tax-free earnings. Pre-tax earnings. After-tax earnings. For the full year 1962, XYZ Corporation announced earnings of $1.35 per share, including a capital gain (nonrecurring) of .03¢ per share, and a certain portion of earnings reflecting an undisclosed amount of "tax credit."

The stock of XYZ was selling at $32.00 per share at the time of this announcement (spring of 1963). The stock was at 24 times earnings, and the holder of that stock was in an awkward position.

Investors value stock on the basis of their earnings—meaning the profits realized from the principal operating section of the corporation after payment of all expenses. Part of the expense of doing business is paying taxes, so it is "after-tax" earnings that have meaning. Assume that the $1.32 (adjusted for .03¢ capital gains) was the normal after-tax earnings of the corporation. Then investors would realize that, from its services and manufacturing operations, the company had netted approximately $2.60 per share and paid the Government its due. Investors could then look forward to watching sales and margins of profit for any changes that might indicate growth or weakness in future earnings. At least they would have a yardstick for measurement.

In the case, however, of a tax credit carry-forward (a credit granted by the Internal Revenue Service to the corporation for losses incurred in previous periods, which are tax allowances against future income earned within a fixed period of time) the investor does not know without research how much the company actually would have earned under normal conditions. Thus, if the company did not have a full tax credit against all of the $1.32, it would have shown earnings *after taxes* of approximately 64¢ per share. The reasoning behind this is that, when the tax credit is used up or expires, the corporation will be faced with the normal expense of paying taxes. So that, if operations at the current level are only producing an equivalent of 64¢ per share, the stock is selling at an adjusted price earnings ratio of almost 50 times earnings. This price level leaves the investor very vulnerable to price declines, because the company will have to *double* its earnings to realize the same figure it is currently showing of $1.32. This is a difficult task for even the finest growth company, and it imposes a severe burden on the earnings capability of this corporation.

(*Note:* The amount of the tax credit is often not reported and must be computed from previous financial reports.)

Tax-free earnings are of great importance to the Undervalued investor because he very often investigates and buys stocks of corporations that have shown losses in previous periods. The company that has lost money has the right to apply those losses against future earnings. When Standard Fruit and Steamship Company lost $7.60 per share in 1960, they opened the way to receiving tax-loss credits when and if they returned to profits. If, as happened, the company showed earnings of 27¢ in 1961, those earnings were *in effect* pre-tax earnings. When, in 1962, the Standard Fruit Company showed earnings of over $5.00 per share, these also were almost wholly tax-free earnings. The significance of the loss carry-forward, or "taxless" earnings, in the price of the stock lies in the fact that the market will value the stock on an adjusted earnings basis. Therefore, if Standard Fruit and Steamship is valued at seven times earnings, the stock will not sell at $35.00 (7 x $5.00) per share, but closer to $17.00 (7 x $2.50).

Until the company returns to a normal basis—i.e., the tax credits are completely used up—then all earnings will have to be adjusted to reflect what the true earnings would have been under the usual tax basis.

Pre-tax and After-tax earnings

Pre-tax earnings are not usually of significant interest to investors, because such earnings offer a distorted view of the profit capability of the corporation. All reference to the earnings of a corporation are normally "after-tax" earnings. When earnings are discussed or reported "pre-tax," the report is or should be clearly designated as such.

When earnings are reported, they are or should be after-tax earnings, unless the qualification "before provision for Federal Income Taxes" or "Giving effect to tax credits" is included in the report.

The payment of taxes is an expense of doing business, just as real an expense as wages and salaries.

There are, however, changes in the capital structure of a corporation that can affect taxes and therefore earnings. One such change in capital structure would be the retirement of a preferred stock issue and the substitution of a bond issue.

Because dividend payments are not deductible, they are paid from after-tax earnings. Thus, if a corporation has outstanding 100,000 shares of 5 per cent preferred stock par value $100, the company is obliged to pay out $5.00 per share, or $50,000 per year, in dividends to the holders of that stock. Because this payout is after taxes, the company must earn $100,000 in pre-tax earnings to cover this obligation.

If the corporation can "call" for the redemption of the preferred issue, thereby paying each holder $100 plus accrued dividends, and then offer for sale an issue of 5 per cent bonds, the corporation would effect savings of approximately $50,000 per year. *Interest* payments on the bonds are an expense item which is paid from pre-tax earnings and is deductible from taxable income.

Though this is oversimplification of the case, the principle outlined forms a significant part of the consideration of all corporations in setting up its long-term financing. There are often enough advantages in the preferred stock issues to override the disadvantages of substituting the bond form.

Index